MINDFULNESS COACHING

Have Transformational Coaching Conversations and Cultivate Coaching Skills Mastery

SATYAM VERONICA CHALMERS

Website: www.mindfulnesscoaching.com.au

For print or media interviews with Satyam please contact satyam@mindfulnesscoaching.com.au

ISBN: 978-1-54391-506-8 (print)
ISBN: 978-1-54391-507-5 (ebook)

Cover Design:
Atol Dupuche from Creative Marks Studio
www.creativemarksstudio.com

TABLE OF CONTENTS

ABOUT THE AUTHOR
Satyam Veronica Chalmers

Satyam first discovered coaching in 2000 and started up her practice. Since then she has been coaching as well as training, mentoring and assessing coaches on a full-time basis. She has trained hundreds of individuals in coaching skills, including working with various large organizations to create an internal resource of coaches. She is qualified as a Professional Certified Coach (PCC) with the International Coach Federation.

From 2008-2011 she held the position of Global Head of Training and Development for Neuroleadership Institute (formerly Results Coaching Systems). This role included heading up a global team of over 100 coach trainers, mentors, and assessors. She was responsible for the development, design, delivery, and evaluation of coach, mentor, and assessor training, and train-the-trainer programs.

In 2002, Satyam completed her first 10-day silent mindfulness meditation retreat, after only meditating sporadically. She was so blown away by the impact this mindfulness technique had on her wellbeing that she went back and did the retreat another five times over the following year. Since then, she has made the practice of mindfulness the primary focus in her daily life, including travelling to India many times to experience different forms of meditation.

Since 2008, she has been successfully supporting her clients to develop mindfulness, as well as facilitating training programs to support coaches to practice and apply mindfulness within coaching. You can find out more at www.mindfulnesscoaching.com.au

Satyam lives in Brisbane, Australia with her graphic designer partner Atol, who created this book cover. They live in an old renovated church where they enjoy running workshops, yoga and meditation.

FORWARD

Are you in a space in your own life where you know there is a much deeper space from which to live and experience life - a space so rich, so wondrous, yet so raw and vulnerable that only the brave of heart dare venture there?

This is the space I found myself in when I decided to participate in Satyam's Mindfulness Coaching training. This is also the space many of my coaching clients are in when we engage.

I met Satyam back in 2001 when I undertook Intensive Coach Training with Results Coaching Systems. Satyam was a trainer with Lisa Rock for the program. That three-month training placed me in good stead to go forth and establish myself as a masterful coach, and I've sustained a full coaching practice since then.

Being a successful coach means considerable commitment, passion, and dedication to championing the success of your clients. Both Satyam and Lisa modelled the coaching competencies with finesse and genuine concern.

With the training behind me and a thriving coaching practice, Satyam and I nurtured a friendship. My children were young at the time, and Satyam (lovingly known as Sati-yum-yum by my children) soon became a part of our family. We all love Satyam, but my son Harrison has and always will have a particularly fond connection with her – truly beautiful to see.

As the years progressed, Satyam undertook her own professional development path with vigour. She completed counselling training and then deep dived into the world of mindfulness. She worked as Head of Training and Development for the Neuroleadership Institute (formerly Results

Coaching Systems) for 3 years and was given an introduction to the world of neuroscience.

Satyam soon devoted countless days, weeks and months to the development of a tailored mindfulness training specifically targeted for coaches. Having herself attained PCC accreditation with the International Coach Federation (ICF), Satyam has a proven track record of accomplishments and expertise as a coach. In fact, Satyam played a pivotal role in mentoring me as I prepared for my MCC accreditation, the highest level of accreditation with the ICF, in 2005 and I've sustained that accreditation to date.

When ready to launch, Satyam called me and asked if I'd participate in the live virtual Mindfulness Coaching training program. Initially, I reluctantly said 'yes, sure'. Having myself completed executive masters studies in Neuroleadership, I mistakenly believed that I had that base covered. Boy was I wrong!!!

The theory was clear and straightforward, with lots of experiential learning opportunities both on the calls and homework practices with learning partners. It looked easy enough, so I volunteered to do a role-play on the live forum, believing I had it nailed and I'd be awesome. Hmmm, not the case at all! The participant I role-played with was going through a rough time in her life, and I approached the conversation with the backdrop of my coaching studies and usual coaching approach. This clearly did not work! No matter what I tried, the conversation was stilted and awkward. Our frustration levels were escalating. When the role-play was finally over, my internal narrative ran something like this: 'How embarrassing. I've just made a fool of myself in front of 20 peers. I don't understand what's going on! I'm doing all the right things and coaching her to move through her experience, but it's not working. This doesn't happen to me. I'm a master coach. I have a successful track record.'

What a powerful learning experience for me! What happened was what we are 'trained' to do in coaching – I facilitated the conversation as a coach, but without the 'mindfulness' component which calls for a deeper level of presence. What was needed was an emphasis on who and how I was BEing for her, rather than the focus on the process. It was a complete un-programming of what I'd learned to become a successful coach and a reprogramming in how to pay sensitive attention and listen for much deeper cues for even more powerful and transformative coaching conversations to occur. It was less about the process of coaching, or what I was doing as a coach and much more about how I was BEing for my client. It was also about listening for information about the emotional journey a client is traversing, rather than only assisting the client to execute tangible outcomes.

What I learned was that by focusing far more deeply on the emotional journey, and listening mindfully for the 'fuel' beneath the journey, clients can achieve so much more by focusing on 'who' they must BE rather than 'what' they must do.

This was a complete world spin for me. I'd attained global recognition and awards for my coaching achievements, and now I was being teleported into a whole deeper level of even more powerful coaching potential.

After integrating the lessons of this experience, I bravely and willingly opened my mind and heart to this new way of mindfulness coaching. As a consequence, I'm loving the coaching experiences even more (I never thought this could be possible as I've been so passionate about coaching, my clients and the industry since day 1), and my clients are reaping the benefits too. The nature of my questions has changed, and I'm listening in a more expanded way.

The mindfulness coaching approach takes practice and patience… but let me assure you, it's a journey worth taking to create a more empowered, compassionate and loving world.

I personally want to thank Satyam for this opportunity to vulnerably share a taste of my own journey with her mindfulness coach training. I encourage coaches who are committed to deeply transforming their own lives and the lives of their clients to read this insightful book and participate in the mindfulness training.

I'm so grateful for the opportunity to have learned these practical mindfulness coaching skills – techniques I continue to practice every day. I applaud Satyam for her devotion to making a bigger positive difference by sharing this book and the Mindfulness to Coaching Mastery Program. I pray that together we will join more mindfully as coaches to create a better world.

Josie Thomson, MCC (ICF Master Certified Coach)
Chief Inspirations Officer, JosieThomson.com
Author: The Neuroscience of Strategic Leadership, Simple Meditation for Busy People, and Enliven-U

INTRODUCTION

Since I started coaching and training coaches, I have seen that the one skill that makes the difference between a good coach and a great coach, is coaching presence. Masterful coaches can stay in the moment with the client, listen at a whole new level, easily tap into their intuition, and communicate powerfully. They support clients to have transformational conversations that shift perspective and create real, lasting change.

At the time I started coaching, I also discovered mindfulness. I did my first ten-day, meditation retreat and came out completely transformed. There was a moment about halfway through the retreat when I realised how much my mind created suffering and that I had a choice about whether to suffer or not. With this awareness came a profound sense of peace and joy.

Soon after this first retreat, I went to India for the first time. I immersed myself in the chaos of India, staying in ashrams to connect more deeply with myself, experiencing a multitude of different types of meditations and therapy workshops. It was an awakening experience of opening my heart fully to life and fully surrendering to existence.

Towards the end of the trip, we had an opportunity to take on a spiritual name, as a way to continue committing to this path of meditation. This name was a way to remind us to stay true to ourselves, even when it becomes challenging within everyday life. The name I was given was 'Satyam Vinya'. Satyam means 'truth' and Vinya means 'discipline'. This name was perfect for me and resonated at a deep level of my being.

Mindfulness is a commitment to truth, to the discipline of staying here in the moment with what is true. The name quickly caught on and has been a powerful reminder on a daily basis to stay true to myself and come back to connect with myself whenever I feel I have been swept away by my stories about the past or future.

Since then, mindfulness has been a daily practice, both on the cushion and within every moment of the day, to support me to be mindful. Mindfulness is an easy enough technique to learn, however, it is much harder to sustain and practice. The mind is often referred to as the monkey mind, jumping all over the place. It takes time, focus, and practice to be mindful, particularly in very stressful situations. However, we are now discovering, through breakthroughs in science, that we can retrain our brains, create new connections, and embed those new connections until they become hardwired. So with practice, mindfulness becomes a hardwired habit.

Of course, as a coach and seeing the benefits mindfulness has given me, I wanted to share this with my clients. So over the years, I have been introducing and supporting clients to develop mindfulness. It has been almost magical to see how this simple practice has transformed their lives. When both coach and client can be mindful, it adds a whole new dimension to the coaching. However, the real joy is in seeing my clients share their presence with others.

In 2008, I started sharing mindfulness with other coaches who have discovered the multitude of benefits for themselves and then shared this with their clients. I have had the absolute pleasure through my virtual program, 'Mindfulness to Coaching Mastery', of connecting with coaches from around the world, coming together to support each other to be mindful. All of these coaches are kind, generous, supportive individuals, committed to making a difference in the world. Through developing their coaching presence using mindfulness, they discover how much greater an impact they can have through coaching.

This book has originated from the work I have been sharing with clients and coaches. It is designed for coaches interested in developing a greater level of coaching presence and at the same time, understanding how to share this powerful tool of mindfulness with clients. I have incorporated the International Coach Federation's (ICF) 11 core competencies within this book. Many of the skills referenced in this book are related to the ICF Master Coach Certification (MCC) level of coaching.

My intention in writing this book is simply to share this powerful tool with coaches so they can share it with clients. Clients will then be able to share their presence with the people in their lives, thus eventually creating a world full of people practicing mindfulness every day. I believe this would create a more peaceful, loving, compassionate, kind world in which to live.

I hope you enjoy reading the book, applying the skills of mindfulness to your coaching practice, and sharing this gift with your clients.

Finally, I want to thank all the amazing kind-hearted generous coaches that contributed to this book by participating in my programs and encouraging me to share this work. I have loved every minute with each of you and thank you for making such a big difference in the world through your presence.

Yours mindfully,
Satyam Veronica Chalmers
ICF Professional Certified Coach
www.mindfulnesscoaching.com.au

Note: The spelling in this book is mostly based on UK spelling. I'm Australian, so this is the spelling I grew up with and still use. I have sometimes used US spelling when it made more sense, however, for the most part, the text is UK spelling.

CHAPTER 1

SCIENCE & PRACTICE OF MINDFULNESS

What is Mindfulness?

The practice of maintaining a nonjudgmental state of heightened or complete awareness of one's thoughts, emotions, or experiences on a moment-to-moment basis. - Merriam-Webster Dictionary

The state or quality of being mindful or aware of something.
- Dictionary.com

The practice of being aware of your body, mind, and feelings in the present moment, thought to create a feeling of calm. - Cambridge Dictionary

Mindfulness is the basic human ability to be fully present, aware of where we are and what we're doing, and not overly reactive or overwhelmed by what's going on around us. – Mindful.org

Mindfulness means maintaining a moment-by-moment awareness of our thoughts, feelings, bodily sensations, and surrounding environment. - Greater Good Science Center at the University of California at Berkeley

1

Mindfulness is being present in the moment in an accepting, open, and non-judgmental way. It's about being able to feel, sense, and see what is happening around you and within you in the moment. Often we are so distracted ruminating about the past and future, lost in a story constructed by our minds that we lose connection with our surroundings and ourselves.

We go into a 'default mode' of worrying, stressing, judging, criticising, planning, remembering, and disconnecting from what is happening in the moment. This is the nature of the mind, so there is nothing wrong with this habit. In fact, some of this default mode can be useful, like when you are planning for an upcoming meeting. However, our minds naturally click off when we aren't engaged and present in the moment. When we spend a good portion of our day in this default mode, we tend to start feeling less engaged with life and more stressed.

A simple example of being in default mode and lost in the rumination of the mind is driving a car on a regular route, arriving at your destination, and not remembering much about the journey. Or walking down a street and missing the birds singing, the sunshine on your face, the anxiety in the pit of your stomach, or the smile from a stranger. Perhaps you've been lost in thinking about the meeting you had earlier in the day, what you need to cook for dinner, the presentation you're giving tomorrow, the argument you had with your spouse, or how you're going to find enough time for yourself this week. Unfortunately, you have completely missed being present and the multitude of benefits that come from being able to stay in the moment.

Focus on the Past and Future

We're often lost in default mode, ruminating about the past and the future. For example, you're on holiday. You've been saving up and looking forward to this holiday by the beach for months. You get to the hotel and immediately decide to go for a walk on the beach. When you first get to the beach, you can feel the sand between your toes, hear the sound of the water, smell the sunscreen, and experience the joy of being on holiday. However, this is a temporary state, and before you know it, you're lost in rumination. Perhaps you see someone that looks like a previous boss. This thought then leads to thinking about how you dared to leave that job and how you need to stop procrastinating about building your business. This then leads to thoughts about how you need to do more marketing and connecting with potential clients, but you're unsure of the best way to do that. Then you remember a webinar you need to watch about marketing. Maybe you should watch it when you get back to the hotel, as well as check to see if there are any urgent emails for work, and so on and so on.

Before you know it, you have forgotten about being at the beach, even though this is the trip you have been working for and looking forward to for the past few months. Instead of continuing to relax in and enjoy the moment, you have started to experience tension because you're thinking about the past and future.

Mindfulness is about supporting yourself to stay in the moment, rather than spending too much time in default mode. It isn't about judging yourself for going into default mode, but instead, it's about choosing to be fully engaged in the present moment.

Difference Between Mindfulness and Meditation

Mindfulness is a form of meditation. Mediation is an all-encompassing term to describe practices that support individuals to reach heightened levels of consciousness. There are many types of meditations, including visualisation, contemplation, yoga, Tantra, and open awareness. Mindfulness is the type of meditation practice whereby you bring your full attention to an object, like the breath or body, as a way of training the mind to be in the present moment, rather than in default mode.

The Science of Mindfulness

For centuries, spiritual gurus from around the world have advocated the benefits of meditation and mindfulness practice. Science is now catching up, proving that mindfulness practices have a multitude of physical and psychological benefits.

Richard Davidson[1] is one of the pioneers in studying the effects of mindfulness practice. In the early 90s, he went to the Dalai Lama requesting support to study some of the monks in the Northern Indian Hills who had been meditating in almost isolation for 15-40 years. Many of these monks had completed 10,000 to 40,000 hours of meditation practice. Davidson wanted to find out how the brain changes after someone has been practicing mindfulness for an extended period.

Unfortunately, on his first trip, he was not able to convince any of the monks to undergo his tests, as they felt that measuring the effects of meditation was useless. They told him that you couldn't study something that was formless and that you just needed to meditate to see the benefits. The monks were right: unless we practice, we can't know and experience the benefits. However, it is still interesting to see the benefits of mindfulness meditation that are showing up through the use of new technology.

Davidson was eventually able to find some long-term meditators in Western countries that were more open to and interested in measuring the effects of mindfulness. Many of these meditators learned to meditate in the Eastern tradition and had come back to the West to continue their practice.

He found that meditators had a greater level of activation in the parts of the brain that were responsible for:

- focusing attention,
- regulating emotions,
- processing sensory information,

---

1 Davidson, Richard. *The Emotional Life of the Brain* (2012)

- self-awareness,
- empathy,
- compassion,
- optimism, and
- resilience.

These meditators have a greater ability to calm themselves down when triggered by strong emotions like anger, fear and anxiety. They can focus their attention in the moment, an ability linked to the prefrontal region of the brain, rather than being caught in emotional reaction or other distractions. They also are more aware of themselves and sensory information. Davidson particularly noticed that the left, prefrontal part of their brains was more activated, which is linked to greater levels of optimism and resilience.

He also did experiments with short-term meditators with only eight weeks of mindfulness training. These results showed increases in the ability to focus attention, regulate emotions, demonstrate self-awareness, and process sensory information. He tested immunity with this group and found that participants had a greater level of antibodies after being injected with the influenza virus than the control group (who had no mindfulness training)[2].

Other scientists, like Dr Craig Hassed[3] from Monash University, have been focusing on the physical and psychological effects of short-term meditation practice. In the book he co-authored with Dr Stephen McKenzie, *Mindfulness for Life*, he discusses how meditation is shown to have the following benefits:

- depression-relapse prevention,
- reduced anxiety, panic disorder, and stress,
- improved emotional regulation,

---

2 Davidson RJ, Kabat-Zinn J, Schumacher J, Rosenkranz M, Muller D, Santorielli SF, Urbanowski F, Harrington A, Bonus K, Sheridan JF. *Alterations in brain and immune function produced by mindfulness mediation.*

3 Hassed, Craig. *Know Thyself* (2008).

- greater emotional intelligence,
- management of addictions,
- better sleep,
- better control and less avoidance,
- preservation of brain cells,
- enhanced attention and self-regulation,
- pain management,
- symptom control,
- coping with a major illness, like cancer,
- hormonal changes, and
- reduced incidence of illness.

Hassed developed a new performance curve, showing that stress isn't necessary to achieve peak performance. Instead, when you're in a calm, mindful, focused space, there is very little or no stress and a high level of performance. This state is what athletes report as being 'in the zone,' focusing on the present, not thinking about the past or future performance, being in the here and now, engaged fully in the moment. The stress that many of us feel often comes from our preoccupation with the past and future.

Another expert in the field of mindfulness, Dr Dan Siegel,[4] wrote a book called 'Mindsight'. His work on mindfulness originated from the case of a young child who had become mute after her mother had been in a car accident. After the car accident, the mother became distant, disconnected, inattentive to her daughter, and easily triggered into a reaction. Before the accident, she was a loving, kind, and attentive parent. Dr Siegel became interested in the middle, prefrontal region of the brain that had been damaged. As a result, he discovered that this part of the brain was responsible for functions like:

- regulating the nervous system,
- regulating emotions like fear,
- empathy and attuned communication,
- insight,

---

4 Siegel, Dan. *Mindsight* (2009).

- intuition,
- response flexibility, and
- morality.

He was fascinated to discover all these qualities showed up in long-term meditators and parents who have raised happy, healthy children.

Stress Response

One of the main benefits of practicing mindfulness is the increased ability to deal with stress. There is a part of the brain called the Limbic System, which is triggered when faced with a perceived threat. If you're in the wilds of Africa and are confronted by a lion, your heart will start to beat faster, you will start to sweat, and blood will be pumped to your muscles. While the body prepares to flee the attack, you become very present as you look for a way to escape. This is a normal activation response to an impending threat, so you can protect yourself by fighting, fleeing, or freezing. After the threat has passed, and you have managed to reach safety again, the body goes back to normal and the response is no longer activated. This response is designed to be occasionally switched on when we need it and then turned off when we no longer need it. This is a useful response because it can mean the difference between life and death.

In our current lives, it is rare we will face a real threat, like a lion, though we often create threats in our minds and experience them as if they were real. We wake up at 3 am worrying about the next day or something we imagine might happen in the future. There is no threat in our environment at that particular moment (in fact, you are likely lying in a comfortable bed, surrounded by the quiet of the night). However, our body experiences the threat as real, and acts accordingly, by responding the same way it would had it been faced with a lion. All the chemicals are released in the brain and body to deal with the threat, however, with nowhere to go and nothing to do. Unlike when we run from a lion, the chemicals are not being used to flee the attack. This activation isn't going to save our lives. Rather, it is likely to keep us feeling stressed and end up making us ill.

Throughout the day we often activate the stress response through our nev-er-ending to-do lists, responsibility for others, and being bombarded by information, emails, social media, and phone calls. Our lives have become full of distractions, which can activate, sometimes at a very subtle level, the stress response, and we often get to the end of our day feeling exhausted.

Through repetitive activation of the stress response, we hardwire our brains for frustration, anger, depression, irritation, and negativity. When we chronically trigger the flight, fright or freeze response, we cause wear and tear on the body.

Our memory and prefrontal region of the brain is most affected by this stress response. The prefrontal area of the brain often referred to as the CEO of the brain. It is more activated when we make decisions, remember information, plan, reason, manage emotions, focus attention, and learn. When we are stressed, this part of the brain is less activated, and thus it is harder to manage all of the above functions.

At the same time the limbic system - particularly the amygdala - becomes more activated, making us more wired for stress and less wired for think-ing. This makes sense when faced with a lion as we rely on this automatic response in these situations. However, in everyday life where we depend on our ability to make decisions, remember, plan, reason, and learn, we need to activate the prefrontal region. Studies have shown that the amygdala shrinks and the prefrontal region of the brain are more activated in those practicing mindfulness.[5]

Mindfulness supports us to discern between what is a real threat and an imaginary one. It supports us to notice when the stress response has been activated and catch it earlier before we are totally in its grip. We can notice what drives this stress response, unhook from the internal dialogue, and redirect our attention to the present moment.

---

5 Adrienne A. Taren, J. David Creswell, Peter J. Gianaros, *Dispositional Mindfulness Co-Varies with Smaller Amygdala and Caudate Volumes in Community Adults (2013).*

Many mindfulness practices are focused on awareness of the breath and body. Being aware of the body is useful in noticing when the stress response has been activated. The breath is usually the first to become restricted, and then our body starts to contract, and we start to feel tension. If these sensations in the body go unnoticed, we might eventually have a panic attack or become unable to move due to back pain. Noticing the breath and the body is a useful way to monitor the stress response.

Negativity Bias[6]

As you begin to practice mindfulness, you might notice how negative the mind seems to be. We often identify with negative thoughts. This is a natural tendency that was developed as a way of surviving. Our tribal ancestors evolved a negativity bias to deal with external threats. If our ancestors looked into the distance and decided an object looked like a lion, they had a greater chance of survival if it turned out to be a lion. If it was a rock, then there was no loss of life. However, if they were being positive and assumed that the lion was a rock, then they would probably lose their lives and have less of a chance to pass on their genes to another generation. They would err on the side of negativity as a result, to keep themselves safe, and thus passed on this negativity bias to the next generation.

We still have this negativity bias today, which can be very useful, as it protects us and ensures we search out ways to provide ourselves with shelter, food, warmth, and safety to survive. However, this default mode of negativity also activates the stress response. We become judgmental, critical, and stressed about everything in our lives, rather than being able to see the real threats. Mindfulness supports us to be aware of this negativity bias, and then we have a choice about where we would like to focus our attention.

---

6 Dr Rick Hanson, *Hardwiring Happiness* (2015).

Mindfulness Practice

The practice of mindfulness is noticing you have been distracted, most likely with repetitive thoughts about the past or future, and then repeatedly bringing your awareness back to the present moment until it becomes an embedded way of being.

Although mindfulness is a simple idea, it is harder to apply in practice. There are many challenges, however, it does get easier with practice, just like when learning to play a musical instrument where you practice over and over again, and then finally master the instrument. By repeatedly returning your attention to the present moment, both in formal and informal mindfulness practice, you will start to notice yourself being more mindful throughout the day.

This repeated focus of noticing when the mind has gone into default mode and then focusing your attention back into the present is rewiring the brain for mindfulness. The brain is creating new neural connections which are embedded through repetition, thus getting stronger.

As you turn your attention away from the default mode and spend less time there, these neural connections weaken. You will still spend some time each day in default mode. However, this reduces over time. Also, it will be easier to notice when you've gone into default mode and thus easier to bring yourself back to the present moment.

The key is supporting the brain to create new wiring for mindfulness by repeatedly bringing your attention back to the moment. At first, when practicing mindfulness, you might notice that you're only able to bring your attention back once or twice in 10 minutes of practice. Try not to be discouraged or judge yourself because you're still developing the new wiring. With more practice, you will notice you're able to bring yourself back more often within in the 10 minutes.

Use the following exercise to practice bringing your attention back to the moment. Spend a few minutes reading through the following transcript and then a few minutes practicing.

PRACTICE: Focus on the Breath

Begin by finding a comfortable position for your body. Close your eyes and take a deep breath, inhaling deeply and exhaling. Allow yourself to slow down and relax. If sleepiness arises, give yourself a gentle message to stay alert and attentive. Be aware as you relax and go inside.

Now, focus your attention on your breath and watch your breathing. I recommend breathing through your nose, however, if your nose is blocked, it's also fine to breathe through your mouth. You may even notice, over time, that you start to breathe through the nose naturally.

Notice how the breath enters and leaves the body completely beyond your control, entering and leaving totally on its own. Watching the breath, begin to feel yourself falling into its natural rhythm, coming in and going out on its own, each moment a new breath, coming in and going out, rising and falling.

The goal of this practice is to experience the breath without directing or changing it. To simply become aware of how the breath breathes in its own rhythms.

You will start to notice the mind is wandering off easily. You may tell yourself to stay focused on the breath, however, the mind has a habit of wandering into thoughts about what you will do after the practice or other issues you feel the need to think about. Instead of giving the thoughts energy, gently bring yourself back to the breath; let go of the thoughts and return to the breath. This is how you train the mind to be in the moment.

Allow yourself to continue following the natural breath. Notice if it feels light, heavy, full, contracted, expanded, cool or warm. Bring a sense of curiosity to your natural breath. Notice how the chest rises and the lungs fill with air and then watch as you breathe out. Notice the coolness or warmth as the breath enters and leaves the nostrils. If the mind distracts you, gently bring your attention back to the breath.

Continue following the natural breath for a few minutes. Notice when the mind wanders and gently bring your attention back to the breath.

After a few minutes, slowly bring your attention back to the room you're in and the chair you're sitting on. Gently open your eyes when you're ready. There is no need to rush, just allow yourself to come back when you feel ready.

Qualities to Cultivate to Support Mindfulness Practice

The spirit you will need to bring to meditation is one of openness, discovery and seeing. To sit, to walk, and to train yourself to bring your attention back to the present moment. To learn the patterns of body and mind that cause suffering, and discover release from that suffering.

– Jack Kornfield, *Meditation for Beginners*

Non-judgmental Compassion and Friendliness

Learning to develop mindfulness is a bit like training a puppy. Each time the puppy wanders away, instead of yelling at the puppy, we want to approach it with non-judgmental compassion and friendliness. If we yell at the puppy to come back, most likely the puppy will be frightened and run away. If you manage to get it back, it will feel scared, rigid, and stressed. When you notice the puppy has wandered away, you can gently bring it back to the spot it wandered away from. When you do this repeatedly over time, the puppy will start to get the message and be able to come back on its own, in a relaxed and easy way.

The same applies for when we practice mindfulness. As we notice the mind wandering from the focus of attention, we gently bring the focus back to the object, usually the breath, body, or senses. By repeating this practice over and over again, you train your mind to effortlessly be in the present moment. However, if you judge your mind for wandering and try to force it back, you end up feeling more rigid and stressed. Instead of criticising yourself for something that the mind does naturally (and has been trained to do) simply remind yourself to gently bring your attention back.

Openness and Curiosity

As children, we are naturally curious and open. As we become adults, we tend to lose touch with these qualities. However, we can reconnect and bring this natural curiosity and openness to seemingly mundane objects, like the breath. Mindfulness practice requires we bring a sense of curiosity and openness to whatever arises in our present moment experience. Each moment is different from the previous moment, even though it might seem the same. If we bring enough curiosity to the moment, we will notice the differences.

Beginner's Mind

Often we feel like we need to approach life as an expert. One of the most refreshing ways to approach both mindfulness and life is to adopt the attitude of the beginner. A beginner's mind is more open to learning about the moment and seeing what is new, rather than assuming we know. It is both liberating and refreshing to let go of what we know intellectually and discover new ways to sense and perceive what is happening right now. When we assume we know or feel we have to be knowledgeable, we miss what is happening in the moment. To develop mindfulness, we need to adopt the beginner's mind, treating each moment as fresh and different.

Acceptance

We tend to find it easier to be in the moment when what is arising feels comfortable, however, when we experience an uncomfortable emotion, thought, or body sensation, we tend to push it away, unwilling to accept what is happening, craving a more pleasurable or at least comfortable experience. We can't accept it because it feels uncomfortable.

Developing mindfulness requires that we start to bring acceptance to all that arises whether it is comfortable or uncomfortable. If there is irritation, anger, pain, or tension, you might resent these states showing up in your experience and have a desire for other more comfortable states. It isn't about trying to achieve a particular state, like peace, happiness, or joy. Instead, it is about accepting and being with whatever is arising in the moment.

Non-attachment

It is easy to become attached to particular sensations or experiences. Often when someone starts a mindfulness practice, they have moments of feeling more peaceful or relaxed than perhaps they have for a long time. They start to attach to these experiences every time they practice mindfulness. Instead, what is needed is to practice non-attachment, being present in the current experience, rather than looking for a particular experience.

You may notice as you practice mindfulness that you are attached to certain thoughts, beliefs, perceptions, feelings, or stories about situations or yourself. Mindfulness supports you to notice these attachments or identifications and to loosen your identification, or attachment. It's a bit like when you become engrossed in a movie. Your body can react to it as if it were real. Mindfulness supports you to develop the ability to detach from these identifications and see the reality of the moment instead.

The following poem is from the Sufi poet Rumi, and perfectly depicts the attitude we need to bring to our emotions and whatever is happening in the moment:

The Guest House

This being human is a guest house.
Every morning a new arrival.
A joy, a depression, a meanness,
some momentary awareness comes
as an unexpected visitor.
Welcome and entertain them all!
Even if they are a crowd of sorrows,
who violently sweep your house
empty of its furniture,
still, treat each guest honorably.
He may be clearing you out
for some new delight.
The dark thought, the shame, the malice.
meet them at the door laughing and invite them in.
Be grateful for whatever comes.
because each has been sent
as a guide from beyond.

> — Jellaludin Rumi,
> translation by Coleman Barks

Guidelines for Formal Practice

To begin to meditate is to look into our lives with interest and kindness and discover how to be wakeful and free. We have so many ideas and beliefs about ourselves. We tell ourselves stories about what we want and who we are, smart and kind. Often these are unexamined and limited ideas of others that we have internalized and then gone on to live out. To meditate is to discover new possibilities, to awaken the capacity that each of us has to live more wisely, more lovingly, more compassionately and more fully.

–Jack Kornfield, *Meditation for Beginners*

Developing mindfulness is like learning to play an instrument or speak a different language - it takes time and practice. I remember learning the piano as a child. There were times when I loved it and times when I dreaded having to practice. At times I felt awkward and clumsy and didn't know what I was doing. I wanted to go outside and play instead of putting in the time to practice. However, after a while, I got the hang of it and started to enjoy it.

Mindfulness is like learning to play the piano. You will, at times, feel all the uncomfortable feelings of learning something new. You might not want to practice and will feel confused about whether you're on track. However, after eight weeks of daily practice, you will start to find it easier. There will still be times when you don't want to practice, but you will start to notice you're able to be more mindful every day, you will see the benefits, and thus will have the motivation to keep practicing.

The most effective way to develop mindfulness is to commit to a regular practice of sitting in a quiet space for at least 10 minutes a day, so the mind starts to embed the ability to bring the attention back to the moment. As human beings, we are so habituated to thinking about the past and future that it takes time to train ourselves to focus our attention toward the present moment.

It is also useful to use an anchor to focus your mind. The anchor supports you when bringing your attention back, rather than wandering randomly. The breath is a good starting point because it is always available as a focus. Begin by noticing yourself breathing in and breathing out. When you notice thoughts distract you, bring your attention back to the breath. You could also focus on a specific part of your body, like your hands, which usually buzz with energy. When you notice you have been distracted by your thoughts, gently bring your attention back to this part of the body.

Other types of meditation focus on a candle flame, mantra, beads, or visualisation, however, it is useful to choose something that is always available, such as the breath or a part of your body. This way, you can practice throughout your day, as well as when you're sitting in your formal practice. It will cultivate more of an inner awareness of the body and your internal state.

Some guidelines for your daily practice include:

- Find a quiet space where you won't be disturbed.
- Set yourself up in a space that is comfortable.
- Avoid lying down for the practice as it is too easy to fall asleep.
- Create an altar or vision board, or find a picture or quote that will inspire you to do your daily practice.
- Set the timer for at least 10 minutes and commit to staying there for that length of time.
- Use an audio track to guide you through the process.
- Let those around you know that you will be unavailable for the length of time.
- Choose a regular time of day, one that is easy to commit to and can eventually become a part of your routine. First thing in the morning tends to be the best time for most people because it is usually quiet and the mind is less busy than at the end of the day.

- After you practice mindfulness, spend a few minutes writing about your experience, by reflecting on what you noticed - for example, body sensations, emotions, thoughts, sounds, smells, and tastes. Write down if you felt any resistance. Where did you notice this and what did you notice when you allowed it to be there?

- Discuss with your mentor or teacher any particular challenges you noticed.

Mindfulness practice isn't about holding a state - feeling peaceful and rested, for example. While this is the by-product of mindfulness practice, it isn't the aim. Mindfulness is about being present with whatever arises, bringing acceptance, and being non-judgmental and open to your experience. Sometimes this will be discomfort, pain or resistance. At other times, it will be joy, peace, happiness, love and compassion.

Mindfulness is a practice of self-remembering. It's common to forget to focus your attention, and the mind may wander hundreds of times in 10 minutes. The important part of this practice is to notice when your attention has wandered and to bring it back to the breath, body, or whatever focus is easiest for you. As you do this, you will gradually find yourself staying with the focus of attention for longer periods and being in the present moment longer.

It's not bad to lose your focus, and it's important you don't use this as something to judge yourself. It is a practice that takes time to master. There is nothing wrong with thinking and using your mind. Sometimes thinking about the past and future is helpful to realise what we want or where we might move next in the future. However, if you are constantly fixated on thinking, this can cause unnecessary stress and tension.

One of the best forms of mindfulness practice is the body scan. Spend a few minutes reading through the following transcript and then 10 minutes practicing. You might also like to speak the following transcript into a recording device and play it back to practice the body scan.

PRACTICE: Body Scan

Begin by finding a comfortable position for your body. Close your eyes and take a deep breath, inhaling deeply and exhaling. Allow yourself to relax, going inside, beginning to slow down and relax. If sleepiness arises, give yourself a gentle message to stay alert, attentive, and aware as you relax and go inside.

Now, allow your attention to focus on your breath and begin to watch the breathing. Notice how the breath enters and leaves the body completely beyond your control, entering and leaving, totally on its own. Watching the breath, feel yourself falling into its natural rhythm, coming in and going out on its own. Each moment, a new breath, coming in and going out, rising and falling.

Now, start to bring your attention to each part of the body and notice sensations or feelings in each part of the body. You might notice tingling, itching, pain, lightness, heaviness, warmth, a cooling sensation, or something else. The purpose of this practice is to be curious and notice what is happening without needing to change it. Go slowly and spend a few seconds focusing on each part of the body.

Start by focusing on the toes on your right foot, feeling into each of your toes and noticing any sensations, then bring your attention to the front of the right foot, the back of the right foot, the right ankle, the right shin, the right calf muscle, the right knee, and the right thigh.

Turn your attention to the left toes, the back of the foot, the front of the foot, the ankle, the left shin, the left calf muscle, the left knee, and the left thigh.

If you notice your mind moving away and getting distracted, gently bring your attention back to the body.

Slowly bring your attention to the buttocks, the pelvis, the stomach, the lower chest, the upper chest, the lower back, the middle back, the upper back, and the shoulders.

If you notice your mind moving away and getting distracted, gently bring your attention back to the body.

Now, turn your attention to the right arm, fingers, and thumbs, then the back of the hand, the front of the hand, the wrist, the lower arm, the elbow, and the upper right arm.

Turn your attention to the left hand and all the left fingers and thumb, then the back of the hand, the front of the hand, the wrist, the lower arm, the elbow, and the left upper arm.

Then turn your attention to the shoulders, the neck, the chin, the cheeks, the nose, the eyes, the eyebrows, the forehead, the ears, the back of the head, and the crown of the head.

Then turn your attention to the whole body, from the crown of the head to the toes. See what else arises.

When you're ready, return your attention to the breath and bring your focus back into the room. Then open your eyes slowly.

Start with 10 minutes a day and then gradually increase the amount of time you spend practicing mindfulness. You might want to begin with the body scan and sit afterwards in silence, opening your awareness to whatever arises in the body. Just remember to notice when the mind has become distracted by thinking and gently bring your attention back to the body. Over time you will notice you can sit for longer periods of time and the mind will become increasing quiet, relaxed, and open.

Guidelines for Informal Practice

Formal practice gives you a greater chance of being mindful when you're not sitting in practice. It is much more difficult to be mindful when there are noises and other distractions in the external environment. Ultimately, we want to bring this mindfulness into the rest of our lives, and there are practical ways to practice daily.

Every day is full of routine tasks - such as eating, travelling, taking a shower, brushing your teeth, washing the dishes, getting dressed, walking, and the list goes on. These are all opportunities to practice mindfulness.

Mindfulness practice is anything that supports you to quiet the mind and focus on the present. For example, the next time you're walking down the street, notice the air on your skin, the colours and textures in your surroundings, the light filtering through the trees, the feel of the earth under your feet, the smells, and anything else you sense. Notice your thoughts, and place more focus on what is happening within you and around you now, rather than giving too much attention to thinking. See if you can watch your thoughts as if they are 'clouds passing through the sky'.

Another task you could use as mindfulness practice is washing dishes. Notice the feel of the water on your hands and the smells of the kitchen. Look closely at the plate you're washing as the water slides off it. Notice how your body is feeling and what emotions are present. Be like a child, washing dishes for the first time. Open your mind to noticing and sensing something you have never sensed before. You will be surprised at the peace that can come from washing dishes with presence.

Other tasks that individuals use as their mindfulness practice include gardening, surfing, painting, yoga, Tai Chi, Qi Gong, walking barefoot on grass, and hobbies. Any activities that require your full focus and attention and provide a space to notice your mind wandering and to practice bringing it back to the moment are useful.

Exercise: Everyday Mindfulness

For the next week, pick a daily task to make into a mindfulness practice. Each day, as you do the task, practice being present with your breath, emotions, thoughts, body sensations, and whatever else arises. Notice when your mind wanders into default mode and gently bring it back to the task.

One of the best places to practice mindfulness is while you're eating. You eat a number of times a day, so it's a great opportunity to practice bringing your attention back to the moment. It's common to be distracted while eating by reading, using our electronic devices, or talking to others. Instead, find a quiet space to eat and practice, noticing when your mind wanders and bringing your attention back to eating.

PRACTICE: Mindful Eating

This exercise can be done anytime you eat anything. The purpose is to bring mindful awareness to everything you're eating and using all of your senses. It is best done without any distractions like TV, reading, or talking to another person. Instead, focus on eating quietly and mindfully without interruption.

Before starting to eat, close your eyes for a few moments to feel your breath, the body, and how you're feeling in the moment. If you're feeling stressed, worried, or angry, then allow yourself to feel these emotions, bringing a sense of acceptance to these states.

When you feel relaxed and mindful, open your eyes and start opening up all of your senses. Notice how the food smells and what it looks like. Notice the different colours, textures, lights, and shadows of the food. Spend a couple of minutes smelling and observing the food before eating.

Then, when you're ready, slowly and mindfully start eating. Notice how the food tastes. Chew slowly so you can taste the food fully.

Notice if the mind wanders or wants to hurry the process of eating. Instead, focus on chewing slowing, noticing the taste and sensation of the food. Try to eat even more slowly than you feel is possible.

Take your time eating the food. Notice how you feel after eating the food. You might notice it was a much more enjoyable experience, especially if it's something yummy, like a mango or piece of chocolate! Or you might notice that when you take the time to eat more mindfully that you don't enjoy it. The main idea is to see what arises as you eat.

Mindfulness Journal

It is useful to keep a mindfulness journal to support you to develop mindfulness. The journal will support you to reflect on your experiences as you develop mindfulness. It can be useful to note down points during the day as you notice when you're mindful and when you're not. The more you notice these experiences, the more you will develop mindfulness throughout your day.

It can also be useful to make some space at the end of your day to reflect on what you noticed during the day. Here are some questions on which to reflect:

REFLECTION: End of Day

1. **Formal mindfulness practice:** What did I notice during my formal mindfulness practice? Was my mind busy? Did I notice moments of being fully present? What did I notice about my emotions, bodily sensations and thoughts?

2. **Informal mindfulness moments:** When was I fully engaged and in the moment? How did I support myself to be mindful?

3. **Default/Unmindful moments:** When was I in default mode today? When did I notice myself going into rumination, planning, criticising, and stressing instead of being in the moment? How could I have supported myself to be in the present moment in these situations?

Creating the Environment for Mindfulness

Many of us have busy, hectic lives, without much space for cultivating mindfulness. So as well as focusing on the formal and informal practice of mindfulness, we need to create enough space in our lives to allow ourselves to be mindful. As you develop mindfulness, you will naturally want to create changes in your life that support you to be present in the moment.

Dealing with Distractions

We are wired for distraction. When we encounter novelty - such as an email in our inbox - dopamine, a pleasure-feeling chemical, is released in the brain.[7] Because of this, we tend to search out distractions to make us feel better, especially when we are involved in a task that feels boring or repetitive. However, the pleasurable feeling is usually temporary, and we end up feeling stressed when we are distracted repetitively.

Wherever possible, eliminate distractions that take up time and space, including external noises that prevent you from being focused. Create more quiet space in your life. This might mean shutting down technology more often, creating a space where you can't be distracted by emails, phone calls, or social media.

Scheduling Time for Yourself

Many of us resist taking time for ourselves, judging it as selfish, or believe we have too much to do to take any time out. Taking time for yourself so you can be more present in the rest of your life means you have more to give to others. By setting time aside regularly for yourself to reflect, write, paint, be in nature, focus on a hobby, or practice mindfulness, you deactivate the stress response.

You might need to take an honest look at what you need to do each day and whether some of the items on your to-do list are necessary. Look at the cost of trying to pack everything into each day. Do you need to do all of those things today? Can you create the space and time to go at a slower pace? Perhaps you can take regular breaks, rather than trying to get everything ticked off the list. Ask others to support you, outsource, or delegate tasks to colleagues or family members. You might find that, by focusing on the moment, you are more effective and get more done in less time.

---

7 Kent C. Berridge and Terry E. Robinson, *What is the role of dopamine in reward: hedonic impact, reward learning, or incentive salience?* **Brain Research Reviews, 28,** 1998. 309–369.

Avoid Complex Multitasking

The world we live in seems to be getting faster; we are expected to do more with the little time we have, which forces us to multitask. Simple multitasking, like walking and talking, is easy to do. However, when we need to multitask more complex tasks, like having a phone conversation and emailing at the same time, it becomes harder to be effective in each of these tasks.

Our brains can only focus on one complex task at a time. For example, when writing an email and talking on the phone, we swap our attention between focusing on writing the email and then focusing on the conversation, and then back again. We do it so fast that it creates the illusion we are focusing on two things at the same time, when in fact, we are not. Instead, we are doing two things ineffectively.[8] This switching between tasks increases our stress response, and we start to miss information and make errors. After a day of multitasking, we often feel exhausted and stressed.

To be effective, we need to practice efficient attention switching by being mindfully focused on one task at a time. This reduces the stress response and we function more effectively. In the above example, this would mean leaving the email and focusing on the conversation, giving it your full attention. You will notice you probably feel calmer and able to listen more effectively, and the conversation may not take as long. Then, by giving the email your full focus after the phone call is finished, it allows you to be clear and focused as you write it.

Mindfulness and Procrastination

Mindfulness is also an effective way to overcome procrastination. Mindfulness helps to bring the mind back to the moment, rather than focusing on what might go wrong or the need to be perfect. When we avoid a task or something we know needs to be done, and keep thinking about it,

---

8 Rubinstein, J. S., Meyer, D. E. & Evans, J. E. (2001). Executive Control of Cognitive Processes in Task Switching. *Journal of Experimental Psychology: Human Perception and Performance, 27*, 763-797.

it continues to loop around our minds and creates an internal distraction. Mindfulness helps us unhook our attention and focus on the task at hand.

The Mindful Walk

One of the best ways to create an environment for mindfulness is to go for a mindful walk and explore your senses. As you walk, notice what each of your senses is picking up on. To start tuning into your senses more, you can practice the following mindfulness exercise sitting silently. Then go for a mindful walk, focusing on each of the senses as you walk.

PRACTICE: Exploring the Senses

Begin by finding a comfortable position for your body. Close your eyes and take a deep breath, inhaling deeply and exhaling fully. Allow yourself to relax, to go inside, and relax. If sleepiness arises, give yourself a gentle message to stay alert and attentive as you relax and go inside.

Now, allow your attention to focus on your breath and begin to watch the breathing. Notice how the breath enters and leaves the body on its own. As you watch the breath, begin to feel yourself falling into the natural rhythm of the flow of air coming in and going out on its own. Each moment, feel a new breath coming in and going out, rising and falling.

Now, focus on your sense of hearing. Open your ears and listen for any sounds that come into your awareness, be it somebody speaking, a bird singing, or someone moving in your house. The idea is to completely focus on this one sense for a few minutes.

When you notice a sound, listen to it and then move onto another sound. There is no need to identify what the sound is. Instead, focus on the quality of the sound. Is it high-pitched, or does it have a deeper sound? Get curious about the surrounding sounds.

See if you can listen for the faintest, smallest sound in your environment. Perhaps it is far away or close. There is no need to identify what the sound is or from where it comes. Simply notice it, and then move onto what else you can hear.

Notice when your mind wanders away and gently bring it back to the sounds in your environment. Continue focusing on listening to as many sounds as possible for a few minutes.

Then, when you're ready, focus on your sense of touch. Notice the feel of the fabric of your clothes on your skin, your shoes against your feet, and the feel of the floor. Notice the feel of the air on your skin - is it cold or hot? The idea is to get curious about this sense and become more aware of the sensation of anything touching your skin.

Notice if the mind wanders and gently bring your attention back to your sense of touch. Keep focusing on your sense of touch for a couple of minutes.

Then, bring your attention to your sense of taste. Notice how your mouth feels and what you can taste. Feel your tongue, the upper part of the mouth, the lower part of the mouth, and notice any taste sensations. You can even move your tongue around your mouth to feel what this is like.

Next, bring your attention to your sense of smell. Notice what you can smell in your environment. You might not smell anything to start with, but keep focusing and see what might arise.

Notice if the mind wanders and gently bring your attention back to your sense of smell.

Start to focus on your body and physical sensations. Notice wherever your attention takes you, but stay focused on the body. If you find your mind drifting away, bring it back to the body. Be curious and open to different sensations in the body. You might feel lightness, heaviness, pain, tingling, warmth, or coolness. Notice the sensations and then move onto another part of the body.

Notice if the mind comes in and attaches to the sensation. Gently bring the mind back to the body and move to a different part of the body.

Continue focusing on the body for a couple of minutes.

When you're ready, open your eyes and focus on your visual sense. Start looking around the room. Notice the different objects, colours, textures, materials, light, shadows, and whatever else you can sense with your sight. Simply notice it and then move on, looking at different aspects of the room. The idea is to get curious about this sense and aware of what you're looking at.

Notice if the mind wanders and gently bring your attention back to your visual sense.

Explore for a few minutes and then when you're ready, complete the mindfulness practice. Remember to bring this awareness of your senses into your everyday life.

The Challenges to Developing Mindfulness

Most of us struggle to commit to a daily practice of mindfulness whether it be formal or informal. Instead of saying 'I don't have time', 'It's too hard', or 'It doesn't work', bring a form of inquiry to the resistance you have to mindfulness practice. Be curious about your resistance because all of these excuses are some form of resistance. Start to notice what comes up for you when you think about practicing mindfulness, or notice what happens when you have committed to spending at least 10 minutes a day practicing, but your mind wants to do something else instead.

It's Boring to Practice

We live in a culture that constantly stimulates us with electronic gadgets, noise, a never-ending to-do list, children, family, friends, and so on. Our minds are continually moving from one thing or thought to another. If you sit for five minutes in mindfulness practice, you will notice the mind's capacity to quickly get lost in thought and move into default mode.

Letting go of outside stimulation and bringing your attention back constantly can feel boring. However, as you practice more, you will notice new experiences and sensations that you hadn't noticed before. You will feel calmer and less stressed.

Addiction to Achieving Something

Many of us, especially in Western society, feel a need to establish our self-worth through achievement. As children, we receive the conditioning message that we are not worthwhile unless we are achieving or accomplishing something. This thought is so subtle and unconscious in our psyche that we hardly notice it and think it normal to focus on constant achievement.

Mindfulness practice has no particular outcome. The focus is on letting go of any outcome and just being in the moment. This can contradict our human conditioning because it can feel uncomfortable to sit or practice mindfulness without an objective. Notice if you're avoiding mindfulness practice because you continually feel as if you need to be achieving something, even if it is a state of relaxation. Relaxation is a common side effect of mindfulness practice, however, if you expect to feel relaxed, it will often elude you. Instead, approach it with no expectations. Just go into your mindfulness practice with curiosity and see what arises.

Avoiding Feeling or Sensing

We can avoid our mindfulness practice because we don't want to feel something going on subconsciously. We know that if we sit or stop, we might have to feel what is happening and that can be uncomfortable. It might be that you're feeling angry, sad, powerless fearful, or desire something that is unavailable to you. Instead of stopping to acknowledge it and to feel what comes to the surface, we distract ourselves by getting busy, focusing on our to-do list, eating chocolate, watching TV, talking, and many other distractions.

We avoid it in the hope that whatever is coming to the surface will go away. These mechanisms of distraction might initially numb us into feeling nothing, however, sooner or later, the feelings or sensations will often resurface worse than before. For example, when a driver gets frustrated by traffic delays. They ignore their frustration and project outwards to all the drivers around them as being slow and calling them bad drivers. Then when someone cuts in front of them, they suddenly escalate into full-blown road rage.

By directing our attention to the present moment and allowing ourselves to feel or sense what we have been avoiding, in other words, by facing instead of avoiding what is arising from the subconscious, it loses its power. In a short time, through acceptance and awareness, the discomfort shifts and will eventually dissolve. For example, I woke yesterday feeling anxious and couldn't figure out why. For the first hour of the day I resisted feeling it and instead pushed it away with thoughts of 'I shouldn't be feeling this way' and 'I have nothing to feel anxious about'. I was about to run a group coaching call and was aware I needed to sit with this before the call. So I stopped for only a minute and felt the anxiety, which quickly moved into sadness. I felt the sadness fully, this then shifted into relaxation. I was then present and ready to run the group coaching call.

It may seem illogical to feel something that is uncomfortable, however, if you can feel it without the story about why it is there. Then it will shift and dissolve quickly. Otherwise, we tend to hold onto these emotions for days, weeks and sometimes years.

Avoiding Feeling Pain

We tend to avoid being mindful when we're experiencing pain. This might be physical pain – like back pain - or emotional trauma - like feeling abandoned after an argument with your husband, wife, partner, or child. So once again, we avoid this pain by distracting ourselves with work, TV, manipulating, controlling, yelling, shopping, eating, or taking alcohol and drugs.

When we bring mindfulness to our pain and allow ourselves to feel it fully, it tends to lose its intensity and may even disappear. The resistance to feeling pain often increases its intensity. By taking away our resistance and allowing the pain to be simply there, it is often easier to manage.

Not Good At It

Since we are conditioned from early childhood to focus on achieving and striving toward our goals, it is natural that we would also bring this same focus to mindfulness practice. I remember when I first started learning about mindfulness I wanted to be good at it and be seen as being good at mindfulness practice. I felt like a failure if I spent my daily practice with my mind wandering constantly. However, I learnt that there is nothing to be good at and that the whole purpose of mindfulness is to let go of this need to be anywhere else other than in the moment.

There is no end goal for mindfulness. It is enough to simply notice your attention has wandered and bring awareness to your current experience, as it is, without the need to change it. Often this need to achieve something from mindfulness practice, like feeling peaceful or happy, will prevent you from experiencing these states.

Mindfulness practice isn't easy. Our minds are trained to be busy and follow every thought without awareness. So just like learning anything new, it takes time to develop the awareness required to consistently be mindful. It will be frustrating at first, uncomfortable, boring, and disheartening at times, however, this is part of learning any new skill, so it is important to keep practicing and bringing all your awareness to these uncomfortable places that don't like to fail.

REFLECTION: Notice What is Happening

As you practice mindfulness this week, notice some of the challenges that arise. Are you avoiding a feeling, perhaps discomfort or pain, or does boredom arise during your practice? Are you attached to achieving an outcome, or being good at mindfulness?

See if you can simply be within each of these experiences. Allow yourself to be open, accepting, and non-judgmental of whatever arises, be it hatred, anger, sadness, boredom, physical pain, desire to get to an outcome, self-doubt, or unworthiness.

Notice what happens when you allow all these different emotions to have space, treating them with friendliness. Be patient and experiment to see how these spaces shift and change.

Exercise: Mindful Awareness

From the exercise below, note where you tend to be mindful and where you could bring more mindfulness. This is an awareness exercise, so there aren't any right or wrong answers. It is designed to support you to you notice when you're mindful and when you're in default mode during the day. Through being aware, you will have more choice about where to focus your attention.

Read through each statement and note down whether you tend to be more mindful or in default mode in each situation.

1. I often drive home without being aware of my surroundings (e.g., traffic lights, cars, etc.).

2. I am often unaware of what I'm feeling in the moment.

3. I tend to forget a person's name after I have met them.

4. I tend to rush through my daily tasks without being aware.

5. I tend to break or spill things because I'm not paying attention.

6. I will find myself listening to someone and missing parts of what they have been saying.

7. I swap my attention between different tasks, unable to focus on one thing at a time.

8. I find myself constantly thinking about the past and replaying what happened.

9. I find myself thinking about the future and planning for what might happen.

10. I often don't notice physical tension or stress until it gets painful.

11. I often walk very quickly, lost in thought, without noticing what is going on around me.

12. I often plan my day or think about other things when I'm in the shower.

13. I watch TV, talk, or read while I'm eating.

14. I am unable to switch off thinking about work at the end of the day.

15. I often wake up in the middle of the night stressed and worried.

16.   I feel like I'm often running on automatic each day.

17.   I get so focused on what I'm trying to achieve that I forget about where I am now.

18.   When on holiday, I find myself thinking about work.

19.   I am often unaware of bodily sensations or being connected to my body.

20.   I often feel overwhelmed and unable to focus on the task at hand.

Note at least three areas you would like to be more mindful and consider an action for each. For example, if you would like to be more mindful when eating, set a reminder in your kitchen to remind you to practice mindfulness each time you eat.

CHAPTER 2

THE MINDFUL COACH

Defining Mindfulness Coaching

The greatest gift we can offer others is our presence. When mindfulness embraces those we love, they will bloom like flowers.

–Thich Nhat Hanh, *Moments of Mindfulness.*

Mindfulness Coaching is a type of coaching where the coach focuses on being fully present in the moment, with the client in a non-judgmental, accepting, and open way. Through the coach's presence and the introduction of mindfulness techniques, the client is also supported to be present, so they can access a deeper level of awareness.

This approach focuses on mindfulness being the foundation of the coaching partnership and the primary focus for the coach. As a result, the core coaching skills of building trust, deep listening, asking powerful questions, direct communication and creating awareness arise from a place of presence.

In this way, the coaching becomes more empowering for both coach and client; there is a sense of flow, relaxation, and being in the 'zone' with the client; the partnership is strengthened, and there is a deep trust in the relationship between coach and client.

It is vital that coaches develop mindfulness as a daily practice in their lives so they can easily apply this in a coaching session. When it becomes a way of being, they can be present in the coaching relationship as authentic, relaxed, confident, and in tune with the client. As a result, they're able to support the client to also develop mindfulness.

Mindfulness vs. Default Mode

When a coach is present and mindful in a coaching session, the session tends to have an ease and flow. The coach feels like she's in the 'zone', relaxed and confident in supporting the client to explore. The coach is comfortable with the uncertainty that arises in the coaching conversation and feels connected at a deep level with the client.

The coach notices the subtle nuances of the conversation, the changes of energy, the underlying emotions, and subtle patterns in the way the client expresses themselves, and they can quickly pick up on and trust their intuition. There is also a sense of equal partnership in the relationship. The coach trusts the client to guide the conversation, and the client trusts the coach to support them by holding the space.

Alternatively, when the coach has a busy mind, she is less likely to be consistently mindful throughout the session. The coach might be distracted by what is happening externally in her life, or by what is going on in the session. This distraction means that she will miss crucial nuances in the conversation that could ultimately be the key to supporting the client to move forward in their lives and work.

Transformational Coaching

When we take time to quiet ourselves, we can all sense our lives could be lived with greater compassion and wakefulness. To meditate is to support this inner potential and allow it to come forth into our lives.

–Jack Kornfield, *Meditation for Beginners*

Ultimately, our clients come to us for support to unlock their inner potential and allow it to come forth in their lives. Often clients and coaches focus on the external world of goals and achievement to reach this potential. This becomes an effort, requiring hard work. But our inner potential is already in us, and our work is to bring it forth. It isn't about achieving something or trying to get somewhere while striving toward a goal. It is about accessing this unlimited resource within ourselves and living from that space. Then when we turn our attention to goals, we are more aligned with them. They are realised easily, the journey towards them is enjoyable, and we feel a deep sense of sustained joy when we achieve the goal.

To support clients to access their inner potential, we need to focus on transformational coaching. Transformational coaching assists clients to go within to discover new things about themselves, develop more self-awareness, and to explore the bigger picture of what is happening in their lives. It supports them to shift to focusing on who they are being, instead of what they are doing.

Transactional coaching is focused primarily on the external situation, like solving a problem, achieving a goal or outcome. The focus is commonly on what the client is doing and what they can do to move forward. If the primary purpose of the coaching is transactional, then the impact and value of coaching are limited.

When we focus on transformational coaching (which comes from a base of mindfulness), we support the client to go within and to be more mindfully aware of their experience. This focus enables them to see the bigger picture and to generate a deeper awareness of what is present. The external situation is often a symptom or reflection of something within. By exploring the client's inner world, they develop a greater level of awareness and a clearer idea of how to move forward.

For example, consider a client comes to you with a time management issue. Specifically, there doesn't seem to be enough time to do everything they need to do each day. A coach who focuses on a transactional approach will support the client to create some ideas to solve this issue. The coach might even give the client some ideas about how to manage his or her time. Of course, there is a place for time management tools, and they can be beneficial. However, the lack of time management skills is rarely the core issue.

A coach who focuses on coaching from the inside out will focus on supporting the client to look at what is happening internally that has resulted in this being an issue. The client is more likely to have insight into, or a new understanding of the core issue and how to transform the situation. For example, the core issue could be that by being busy and having a chaotic schedule the client avoids feeling what is going on for him. The client is hiding from listening to what he actually needs, feelings about the life he is living, and what he intuitively senses needs be done to bring it back into balance. No time management tool is going to be effective until the client becomes aware of the imbalance internally and takes steps to bring himself back into balance.

Supporting the client to go within allows the client to acknowledge the core issue. This awareness can shift him into a new way of being and ultimately move forward to achieve his goals.

What Does it Feel Like?

It is useful to become conscious of what it feels like to be fully present in a coaching session, so you can be aware of when you're not present and use the mindfulness techniques to bring yourself back into the moment.

Often coaches report that when they are fully present in the coaching session, they feel:

- engaged,
- in the flow with the client,
- trusting their inner knowing,
- expansive,
- at ease,
- relaxed,
- content,
- open,
- peaceful,
- trust in whatever arises,
- open-hearted,
- compassionate, and
- alive.

On the other hand, when a coach isn't present they may experience feeling:

- awkward,
- doubtful,
- judgmental of self and client,
- pushing to get to the outcome,
- contracted,
- tense,
- closed, and
- distracted.

In particular, you begin to notice the clues in your body. Often we think we are present, however, when we start to sense our body, it tells a different story. Notice if there is any contraction in the body. Is the jaw tense? Is there an ache around the heart? Does the belly feel tight? Is there tension up the spine? Do your eyes feel strained or sore? Is the throat blocked? Are you feeling tension just above the belly and below the chest? These are signs that the nervous system is vibrating with tension, the limbic system is probably activated, making it difficult to be completely present with the client.

REFLECTION: Mindful Coaching Presence

What does it feel like to be mindfully present in a coaching session? What does it feel like to <u>not</u> be mindfully present in a coaching session?

Spend some time reflecting after each session.

Qualities of a Mindful Coach

The coaches who expand my mind, emotions and performance come to the coaching relationship from a place of inner calm. They have quiet minds. They are not beguiled by fancy techniques or elegant coaching models. They are midwives for the narrow, messy emergence into a larger world - and they rely on habits of mindfulness to accomplish that.

– Douglas Riddle[9]

Cultivating a Quiet Mind

The mind is conditioned to be busy. It is often referred to as the 'monkey mind'. Like a drunken monkey that has been bitten by a scorpion and in a chaotic bid to run from its pain, the monkey leaps from tree to tree, frantically seeking relief. It cannot be still, even for a moment.

A mindful coach cultivates a quiet mind through everyday practice, both in and out of the session. Mindfulness becomes a hardwired habit and primary way of being. They will still fall back into the default mode.

---

9 https://www.forbes.com/sites/ccl/2012/01/23/three-keys-to-mindful-leadership-coaching/

However, they notice this quicker and bring themselves back to the present in the moment.

Awareness of Self

Mindful coaches actively inquire within about what is happening internally for them at any time during and after a session. They commit internal inquiry. They're able to differentiate between the client's issues, beliefs, and perceptions, and what is their own. They can notice when something in the session triggers them, and instead of reacting, they're able to respond more powerfully. They are willing to discover new things about themselves, see their blind spots and limiting patterns.

They also understand how their relationship with themselves impacts the coaching relationship. Anything that is unresolved in the coach often shows up in the coaching session, so they need to practice mindfulness to be able to respond in a way that empowers the client, rather than reacting from their unresolved internal issues.

Non-attachment

Coaches are aware of when they're attached to the client achieving an outcome. They also bring awareness to what is motivating their need for the client to achieve an outcome, such as the coaches' need for recognition or to feel valued.

When a coach is attached to achieving a particular outcome, the solution is usually more transactional. The focus is on solving the surface-level issue, rather than transforming the situation and generating a deeper level of awareness. The solution is often based on the clients' or coaches' old thinking, rather than trusting that something new might arise from the conversation.

Many coaches became coaches because they were highly successful in their chosen fields. However, this same focus on achievement and performance can make it challenging to be present in the moment. Many of us want to change what is happening in the moment, and we become very uncomfortable if the client doesn't progress, or move toward achieving an outcome. Our intense focus on achieving an outcome means that we miss subtle conversational nuances that could be the key to clients having the insights needed to move forward.

This approach doesn't mean that we don't set goals, results, or outcomes and focus on achieving them. Instead, it is about noticing our attachment or need for the client to achieve these outcomes. If we can let go of our attachment to the outcome, we can be more present in the moment and often the solution naturally arises in the space.

Relaxing Into Uncertainty

One of the main issues for coaches is the inability to relax into uncertainty during the session. We need to know where the session is going and ensure the outcome will be achieved. The cause of this drive towards results is the need for certainty. It is an essential need for us as human beings, and this is reflected in the coaching session. If we have certainty, then we can relax and feel confident we will achieve the outcome. Unfortunately, manipulating the session to create certainty can inhibit the creative flow of the session to generate new awareness. We need to relax into uncertainty to support the client to create new awareness.

Holding the Space

When coaches develop a deep level of presence in the session, they're able to hold the space for whatever arises for their clients. They can allow clients to express themselves openly in whatever way they choose in the moment.

Holding the space means letting go of the need to fix the client, give them advice, or make judgments about their situation or where they should be. It is a very human tendency to feel the need to do these things, especially as a coach where we might see it as our role to give advice and 'get them' to the outcome. However, this attachment to an agenda reduces the coach's ability to hold the space.

Holding the space also means being aware of your energy and not projecting onto the client. In relationships, it is too easy to project our issues onto others, and this can also happen in coaching. It is important to be aware of our reactions, patterns, and beliefs in a coaching session, so we don't inadvertently project these onto our clients.

The mindful coach creates an emotional space without land mines, where the coachee isn't worried about being manipulated or controlled.

–Douglas Riddle[10]

Co-Creative

Mindful coaches create with the client in the moment. They hold the space for the mystery of the session to unfold, rather than thinking it must go in a particular way, or in a particular direction, or reach a particular outcome.

True creativity is when something arises in the session that neither the coach nor client would have been able to predict. It might be a new idea, awareness, or understanding that comes as a surprise to both parties. It is like the mystery reveals itself in a way that is beyond the clients' knowledge or current perspective of the world and themselves.

Compassion

One of the benefits of mindfulness is that we start to accept ourselves more fully and what naturally arises is a feeling of self-compassion. This self-compassion then overflows to others. We have more compassion and ability to accept where others are at in their lives.

---

10 https://www.forbes.com/sites/ccl/2012/01/23/three-keys-to-mindful-leadership-coaching/

Mindful coaches can share this experience of compassion with their clients. The client feels the compassion from the coach and is then able to have more compassion for themselves. This then strengthens the connection between coach and client.

Living a Mindful Life

Mindful coaches live mindful lives. They don't expect to walk into sessions being mindful and then leave mindfulness at the door at the end of the session. They practice supporting themselves to be mindful and connecting with themselves on a daily basis. They have space each day for connecting with themselves. They allow space between sessions and they don't fill their lives with to-do lists. They know that by living a slower lifestyle, which includes mindfulness practices and quiet time to reflect, they can then more easily coach from a space of presence.

As coaches, we are privileged to serve as midwives to human change - and can impact the performance of entire organizations. How do we contribute to the possibility of change? How do we serve as catalysts for turning experience and reflection into more effective, meaningful lives? Mindfulness offers a powerful alternative to the coercive and linear assumptions that have dominated our thinking. It might be that individual change is not so much driven as permitted. The question for the coach is this: how can I prepare myself to create a mental, emotional, and relational space in which someone may grow and develop? Mindfulness practices prepare coaches to really help instead of just trying to be helpful.

–Douglas Riddle[11]

---

11 https://www.forbes.com/sites/ccl/2012/01/23/three-keys-to-mindful-leadership-coaching/

PRACTICE: Mindful Moment

Take a moment to practice mindfulness. Focus on your breath, your body, and your senses. Notice how you're feeling in this moment: the surrounding sounds, and the colours and textures of the surrounding objects. Bring acceptance to all that is within and around you.

Challenges to Being Mindful in a Coaching Session

Over the years of coaching and training coaches, I have noticed many challenges that prevent us from being fully present in the moment with clients. Just acknowledging some of these habitual thoughts and patterns supports coaches to normalise them and develop a new way of approaching the session with mindful acceptance.

Buddhist traditions of mindfulness meditation refer to two main causes of suffering: our avoidance of experiences that feel uncomfortable, and our attachment to experiences that feel comfortable. If you look at your life, many of your habitual reactions are a way of getting something you want to experience and avoiding something you don't want to experience. For example, it's common to attach to feelings of joy and peace and avoid anger, sadness, and grief.

Some common attachments that make it difficult for coaches to be present include:

- wanting to be seen as competent and confident;
- needing certainty about where the coaching session is going and that the outcome will be achieved;

- being attached to structure, tools, and assessments that create an illusion of certainty;

- being valued, appreciated and liked;

- being knowledgeable and having all the answers;

- feeling like the session is flowing;

- being present - even our attachment to being present can get in the way of actually being present, most likely because we have an image of what being present looks like; and

- needing the client to have insights.

Experiences we may avoid as a coach:

- being seen as ineffective and incompetent;

- being seen as a fake and that the client will find out that you don't know what you're doing;

- tension, conflict, or anger in the session;

- not being liked;

- feeling disconnected and uncomfortable;

- a conversation that lacks direction;

- not feeling like the session is progressing toward an outcome;

- the client deciding to leave the coaching relationship; and

- the client going in a direction you think isn't useful.

The awareness of being attached to, or avoiding an experience in the coaching session is the key to being present in the moment with the client. By being aware, we can better respond in the session by practicing mindfulness, rather than reacting.

REFLECTION: Attachments and Avoidance

Spend some time reflecting after each coaching session on the following questions:

As a coach, what are you attached to experiencing in your coaching sessions with clients? What is the impact of these attachments?

What are you avoiding experiencing in your coaching sessions with clients?

What is the impact of this avoidance?

The very root of these movements of the mind is dissatisfaction. We seem to want both endless excitement and perfect peace. Instead of being served by our thinking, we are driven by it in many unconscious and unexamined ways. While thoughts can be enormously useful and creative, most often they dominate our experience with ideas of likes versus dislikes, higher versus lower, self versus other. They tell stories of our successes and failure, plan our security, habitually remind us of what we think we are.

This dualistic nature of the thought is the root of our suffering. Whenever we think of ourselves as separate, fear and attachment arise and we grow constricted, defensive, ambitious, and territorial. To protect the separate self, we push certain things away, while to bolster it we hold on to other things and identify with them.

– Jack Kornfiled, *A Path of Heart.*

The Inner Judge

Being non-judgmental is an essential part of mindfulness, so it is important to be aware of our inner judge. It isn't about getting rid of the judgment, but rather, about being aware when judgments arise.

What is the Inner Judge?

The inner judge is that voice in our heads that is constantly evaluating everything and everyone, especially ourselves. It assesses what we do, say, and think, and what others do, say, and think. For example, if you're waiting for your new client to arrive and you feel a little anxious, you might notice an internal dialogue along the lines of: 'I hope they like me. I hope the session goes well. Will they sign up for a coaching series? What if I don't ask the right questions, or say the wrong thing? Or, what if I don't get the outcomes their manager has specified?' and so on. This internal dialogue goes on constantly, often repeating the same messages over and over.

Where Does the Judge Come From?

The inner judge tries to protect us. This aspect of our psyche forms during our first few years of life. It developed to keep us safe, so we could fit in and be loved. It's all the voices of parents, grandparents, brothers, sisters, teachers, and other authority figures who have ever given us verbal or nonverbal messages, about how to live and fit into society. Perhaps it was simply a look of disapproval the first time you shouted too loud in a supermarket, being ignored when you started crying or told you needed to be a good girl or boy to be accepted and loved by others.

The inner judge plagues us all with what we can and cannot do. It is the constant voice in our heads that protects us and keeps us safely in our comfort zone, just like our parents did when we were little. Progressively we took these voices into ourselves and internalised them, so we had these voices telling us what we could and couldn't do. For example, we try to fit in, by saying things we believe others want to hear, instead of the truth. We need to do what is expected of us, rather than what we want to do. All of this is an attempt to be liked by others; because we all have an underlying need to be liked and loved.

This isn't about blaming anyone or looking for the cause of these voices. It is about being aware of these judgments as they affect us today, particularly when they arise in mindfulness practice and coaching sessions.

In my first years as a coach, my inner judge constantly evaluated whether I was 'doing it right. Was I asking the right questions, was I listening carefully enough, and was the client getting any value from the session?' I would go into a state of not knowing what to ask next and didn't trust myself. I was ignoring my intuition and trying to coach according to how I thought I 'should' be coaching.

Over time I became more aware of the inner judge voice and was able to loosen my identification with the judgments. I was then able to trust myself more. By this time, I had learned many skills as a coach and could draw on them intuitively, rather than trying to do it 'right'.

Of course, the inner judge is also highly active in our clients. The inner judge stops them from moving ahead and achieving their goals. With awareness, you can start to support clients to notice when they are under attack by their inner judge.

Our Coaching Personalities

Through the identification with the inner judge dialogue, we eventually learn to suppress anything unacceptable and try to create an image based on what others will find likeable. This is why so many people feel like they are faking their way through life, being inauthentic, or feeling like they aren't themselves around others. We identify with this image, as the mask we put on, like a suit, to fit in. The personality consists of all the attributes we would say about ourselves. Perhaps we're intelligent, happy, kind, generous, important, beautiful, energetic, loving, relaxed, content, spiritual, artistic, talented, educated, or responsible. This includes our roles of being insightful coaches, caring mothers, responsible parents, supportive sisters, talented surfers, or knowledgeable doctors. We identify with these roles to present an image to the world.

This image usually covers up the aspects that we reject in ourselves. We don't want others to see us as depressed, moody, angry, lazy, mean, intense, manipulative, controlling, stingy, stupid, ugly, cruel, childish, serious, unsupportive, irresponsible, uneducated, or lacking in talent. We either consciously or unconsciously prevent others from seeing our darker qualities because we think we won't be loved.

As a coach, we need to look at the personality we present to the world and our clients. How does this limit our ability to be fully present? For example, one of the qualities I identify with is strength. As a child, I was acknowledged and praised for this characteristic, so I received the message that I needed to be strong. However, I realised that this could also be a way to cover up feelings of weakness or vulnerability.

This new awareness supported me to start owning this quality by acknowledging when I felt vulnerable. Then I started to see the gift and value in being vulnerable. I noticed that being vulnerable meant others could see the real me.

This acceptance of feeling vulnerable liberated me from having to be strong when I didn't feel like it. At times, I have postponed a coaching session when I felt too vulnerable and unable to support my client. I also have made myself vulnerable in sessions by letting my client know I haven't got it all figured out, and I'm on a learning journey, too. I have noticed this kind of authenticity supports the coaching relationship by deepening trust.

By feeling and acknowledging my vulnerability, I could be more fully present in the coaching session. The key is to acknowledge it (at least to yourself) and feel the part of yourself that you are ignoring.

The reality is that we are everything, all the qualities at some point in time. Often, we choose to express and suppress certain qualities, but by bringing acceptance and mindfulness to all of our qualities instead of rejecting them, the judgment loses power. The inner judge can no longer control us because we have fully accepted these qualities in ourselves.

Judging our Clients

Perhaps we don't judge ourselves, but instead, we notice we judge others. I sometimes hear from coaches I mentor, 'How do I deal with the situation where the client is so verbose, when they are playing the victim in their lives, or when they aren't taking the actions to achieve their goals?'

These questions come from a place of wanting to provide the best value for clients. However, the underlying judgment creates noise in the coaches mind during the session; they get distracted by the inner dialogue and struggle to know what to do under the circumstances.

To begin to learn how to deal with these situations, it is worth considering that judgments about others are usually judgments about ourselves. For example, if you notice you feel frustrated because a client isn't making progress, then you could be judging yourself for your lack of progress.

Judgments inhibit our ability to be fully present. We unconsciously identify with these thoughts during the session and can no longer listen deeply, ask insightful questions, or pick up on the subtle nuances that would move the client forward.

What to do about the Inner Judge?

Step 1 - Awareness

When the inner judge is in action, it feels like we are being attacked. In reality, the inner judge is just trying to keep us safe and protect us from harm both psychological and physical.

Often, we aren't aware of inner judge attacking us. It takes some practice to notice an attack from the inner judge. It is so much a part of us; we rarely notice it working.

The first step is to notice when we're under attack from the inner judge. Here are a few ways to become more aware of the attack.

Bodily Sensations

The body is usually the best place to start. Likely symptoms of the inner judge attacking include a feeling of heaviness in the body, or constriction in the chest or throat, headaches, tiredness, lethargy, weak legs. The idea is to become familiar with the sensations that accompany an attack. For example, I'm aware when I have a headache that I'm likely under attack from my inner judge.

Reflection: What bodily sensations do you notice arising when you're under attack from the inner judge?

Emotions

Emotions are a good indicator of an inner judge attack. Perhaps you feel moody or agitated, are easily frustrated, or you are afraid, shameful, numb, shocked, confused, unhappy, angry, aggressive, or guilty. For example, when I feel irritated by little things, then I know that I'm under attack from my inner judge.

Reflection: What emotions do you notice that are symptoms of the inner judge attack?

Repetitive Excessive Thinking

Notice if you think excessively, particularly in your mindfulness practice. This could indicate that the inner judge is operating below the surface. Notice if you're attached to a particular thought, thinking about something repetitively, or simply notice that your mind is busy and won't settle during your mindfulness practice.

Reflection: What thoughts do you notice are symptoms of the inner judge?

Habitual Compensations

Notice your compensations or ways you avoid feeling. The inner judge is usually in action when we go into these compensations like eating excessively, spending too much time on social media, watching TV, shopping, working too much, sleeping, and taking drugs.

Reflection: What are your habitual compensations?

Judging Others

Another good indicator of the inner judge attacking is when you judge others. This judgment about others is usually a judgment about you. For example, if you're judging someone for being a victim, then check to see if you're judging yourself for being a victim in some area of your life. Notice when you're judging others and bring the judgment back to yourself to see what is there for you.

Reflection: What are your judgments of self and others?

Step 2 - Mindfulness

By bringing mindful awareness to your experience in this moment i.e. thoughts, body sensations, and emotions, then you will notice that the inner judge loses its power. Mindfulness brings a space of openness, acceptance, and non-judgment to the inner judge attack. This provides a space for it to be there, rather than pushing it away or wishing it was otherwise.

The space created through mindfulness quiets the mind, allowing the attack to recede into the background until it no longer has a hold on you. You might notice it is still there trying to draw your attention. However, it lacks any real power over you.

If you notice the attack is still strong or doesn't seem to be shifting, then you most likely are still attached to a story about the judgment. For example, the story about why you're not good enough as a coach or feel like a fake. It can be useful to acknowledge the story, notice the thoughts and then bring your awareness to the body sensations and emotions.

By bringing your attention to your whole experience, rather than just a small segment called the inner judge, you will start to feel it fade into the background. You will start to connect with a deeper truth and recognise the falsehood of these more superficial truths created by the inner judge. For example, when you connect more deeply with yourself, you can recognise that you are enough. It isn't even a thought you need to think; it is an experience that naturally arises from this inner connection.

REFLECTION: Notice the Inner Judge

Start to notice the symptoms of the inner judge attacking. Notice how the attack shows up in your body, emotions, and thoughts. Write down what you notice. See if you can bring mindfulness to what is showing up. Allowing space for whatever arises and notice what happens.

Developing Mindful Awareness

Developing Awareness in the Session

Some of the ways you can support yourself to develop mindfulness during coaching sessions are:

- using a physical anchor or focus like your hands and feet - when you notice yourself being distracted, bring your attention back to your body;

- being aware of feelings like anger and anxiety, and allowing them to be there, rather than trying to resist them;

- using placement and recapping what you've heard or what the main points are in the conversation, allows both coach and client to come back to the present moment;

- slowing down the pace - a fast-paced session is usually an indication that you're not entirely present;

- asking the client what is present for them in this moment - take the opportunity to be mindful in the moment as well;

- using silence to explore what is happening to you instead of thinking about the next question;

- ensuring the environment is quiet and conducive to being present - it's much more difficult for the mind to remain quiet if we have too many noises or distractions around us; and

- going through a mindfulness practice before and at the beginning of the session with the client.

Reaction or Response

As mentioned in the previous chapter, there is evidence that mindfulness improves the ability to respond in a situation instead of reacting. When we are unaware, we tend to react without even realising it. When we become aware of our habitual reactions, we start to have more choice about how to respond.

Learning to observe ourselves and the habitual ways we do things in the coaching session, supports us to be more mindful. Noticing when a habit arises, how it functions, and what the impact is, ensures we can stay mindful as coaches.

A way to observe this is to notice the trigger, your reaction, and then the impact. For example:

Trigger: The client isn't achieving the outcome she had hoped for at the beginning of the session.

Reaction: We start to have certain thoughts, feelings, and bodily sensations as a result of reacting to the trigger. We may begin doubting our skills and think what we are offering is of little value. Perhaps we even project this onto the client, thinking she isn't motivated, or she is too verbose. We might start to get anxious internally as the clock signals we're getting closer to the end of the hour.

Impact: We miss what the client is saying and the subtle nuances that would indicate what direction to go to generate a deeper level of awareness for achieving the outcome.

Response: Alternatively, we respond mindfully in the moment. We notice that the client isn't getting to the outcome she set at the beginning of the session. We notice our internal reaction to this information and at the same time, stay present with the client. We notice our thoughts, feelings and bodily sensations, however, we consciously maintain the intention of staying with the client and to what is and isn't being said. We are more aware of listening deeply and take into account subtle nuances in the conversation that might indicate the pathway to a solution or outcome.

Reflecting on Coaching Sessions

The best way to develop more mindful awareness of what is happening in your coaching sessions is to reflect later on what went well, what didn't go well, and your triggers and reactions.

For example, if the trigger was that time was running out in the session, and the client was stuck. Your reaction was to get distracted, thinking about how to get the session back on track. You also felt anxious that the client might not achieve what she wants. You also noticed a slight contraction in your throat. The possible impact was that the client didn't feel heard and you missed something that could have supported the client to get to insight. Next time, you decide to respond by acknowledging the time, asking the client what would be useful to spend the time on, and then listening deeply to what the client says.

Another example is when the client appears stuck and unable to come up with ideas about how to move forward. The trigger is the client not coming up with ideas to move forward. Your reaction is to create certainty by giving her advice. You notice that you felt uncomfortable with the uncertainty of the moment. You're aware of wanting the client to think you're a competent coach by having lots of information and advice for her. The impact is that the client doesn't feel empowered and the motivation to follow through may not be as strong. Next time, your response might be to ask a question or use clarification to identify what you're picking up on intuitively in the session to support the client to gain a deeper level of awareness.

Even with awareness, you may continue to repeat the same habitual reaction, again and again, before being able to respond differently. Our habits are deeply embedded, however, by committing to being more mindfully aware of our usual reactions or habitual ways in coaching sessions, eventually, we will embed the new response, so it becomes a new habit.

REFLECTION: Coaching Session Review

1. Spend at least 10 minutes after a session reflecting on the session.

2. Write about how you felt in the session. Did the session flow freely or did you feel distracted, frustrated, or stuck?

3. Note any moments in the conversation that worked well - perhaps it was a question you asked or an insight the client had.

4. Note any moments in the conversation that didn't work well - perhaps it was a question that didn't land well with the client, a comment you made, or a feeling that something wasn't quite right.

5. Write about any triggers and reactions you notice within yourself. Identify the emotions, bodily sensations and thoughts you had in the moment. Look at the impact of your reactions, then decide how you would like to respond differently the next time you encounter this trigger.

• CHAPTER 3 •

DEEPENING THE CONNECTION WITH CLIENTS

Connecting Deeply with the Client

A mindful coach can draw a person into a moment of connection in which all distractions disappear.

–Douglas Riddle[12]

The trust, connection, and energy between coach and client are vital for going to deeper levels of awareness with the client. The greater the depth of connection and trust, the more the client's limbic system of the brain (the fight, flight or flee centre) can relax, and the prefrontal region (the ability to think clearly, make decisions, remember, and focus) can make connections, including picking up the signals from the neural pathways in the gut and heart. These signals are subtle and easily overridden by noisy mental chatter and an aroused limbic system.

---

12 https://www.forbes.com/sites/ccl/2012/01/23/three-keys-to-mindful-leadership-coaching/

To provide the client with an experience of coaching that is transformational, we need to delve more deeply into the client's whole experience. If we focus on the surface level of the conversation, we may solve the issue temporarily, however, we won't create sustainable change. For example, a client I recently coached who was micromanaging his team needed to learn how to step back and allow the team to make decisions, act on their own, and make mistakes. However, this was unlikely to happen until he understood the underlying issues, including his need to control others, fear of failure, and lack of trust in others. By understanding and being aware of his internal dynamics, the client was then able to make changes externally with concerning how he managed his team.

To work more deeply with the client, we need to connect more deeply, so we can create a space that feels safe enough to delve into what is going on at a deeper level for the client. An analogy for working at a deeper level is the image of an iceberg. We tend to work with the results and behaviours that are on the surface and easy to see, however, this is only a fraction of the iceberg. We need to explore below the surface of the water to see what is driving the behaviours and results, such as the client's values, perceptions, thinking, emotions, intuition, knowledge, skills, personality, judgments, disowned aspects of self, and so much more. We need to connect to the client's whole being, which includes all of these aspects.

For example, a few years ago I had a participant who was training to be a coach. He was the CEO of a small organisation. He was constantly late to the classes and always made his excuses. It was a running joke with his executive team that he is always late. I coached him about this issue on the second day of training, and he realised that being late was a way of gaining attention, originating in childhood. He realised that unconsciously by being late, he was broadcasting to his team that 'I'm more important than others on the team and my time is more valuable'. By simply being aware of the driver for this behaviour he was able to change it without the need to discuss time management techniques.

Rather than focusing only on fixing the behaviour or results, by acknowledging the underlying dynamics in any situation or issue, it is more likely the new awareness will lead to long-term sustainable change.

Connecting with Self

As coaches, if we want to connect deeply with our clients, then we need to connect deeply with ourselves. Often the depth a client is willing to go to in the conversation is determined by the coach's depth of connection with herself.

An example of this was a coach I mentored a few years ago. She was an executive coach for senior management in large organisations. She noticed a pattern with her coaching clients. For the first few sessions, the client would progress well and create new insights and awareness. They would get to a certain point of insight about themselves with the potential to transform their lives/work, and they would shut down and not want to do anymore coaching, or they wanted to focus back on something easier and less confrontational. When this happened, instead of supporting the client to gently explore what was going on, she supported the client to focus on the surface-level issues, since this felt more comfortable. However, niggling in the back of her mind was the thought that there had been a missed opportunity. Possibly, the client was testing whether it was okay to make themselves vulnerable, deciding it wasn't okay, they would go back to focusing on surface level issues.

As I mentored this coach, I noticed that although she had a commitment to delve more deeply into her internal dynamics, there was a place where she just couldn't go beyond a certain depth of awareness. She was also very uncomfortable expressing emotions, articulating what she was feeling, or making herself vulnerable.

Over the next few sessions, the coach learned to develop more mindfulness, acknowledge some of the ways she protected herself by projecting a particular image, as well as see the places she wasn't willing to make herself vulnerable. By allowing herself to be vulnerable in our sessions, she became more comfortable supporting her clients to delve more deeply into their internal world. The clients also became more comfortable going to a deeper level with her.

To connect deeply with clients, we need to be willing to connect with all aspects of our being, including those parts of ourselves we disown, that feel vulnerable and challenging. Connecting at a deeper level requires us to be open to whatever arises in our consciousness.

Mindfulness supports us to develop deeper levels of connection and self-awareness, as well as taking the time to reflect, go inward, notice when we are triggered, feel our feelings when they arise, and be aware of our body and what it is communicating. We need to be willing to accept, open, and make space for what happens for us internally, bringing compassion and curiosity to our internal world, both within and outside a coaching session.

PRACTICE: Mindful Moment

Take a moment to practice mindfulness. Focus on your breath, your body, and your senses. Notice how you're feeling in this moment, the surrounding sounds, and the colours and textures of the surrounding objects. Bring acceptance to all that is within and around you.

How we avoid connecting

To connect more deeply, we need to become more aware of when we disconnect from ourselves, the client, and the relationship. As human beings, we often protect ourselves from having a deep connection with others, and most importantly, ourselves. We want to protect ourselves from being fully seen by our clients. When we can be more authentic, open, accepting, and loving with ourselves, we have less need for protection, and we can be more comfortable letting the client see us.

Here are some ways we might protect ourselves from connecting more deeply with ourselves:

- excessive or repetitive thinking on a subject/situation,
- attachment to creating or perpetuating drama,
- the need to constantly be planning for the future,
- excessive thinking about the past and what could have been,
- judging ourselves for what we should have done or said,
- beliefs and perceptions about how things should be or are,
- making assumptions about situations or people,
- habitual feelings or reactions to certain situations or people,
- withdrawing, fighting or blaming others,
- holding back from sharing ourselves more deeply, and
- losing ourselves in compensations like food, shopping, TV, movies, sleep, social media, alcohol, drugs, and so on.

Here are some ways that we might protect ourselves in a coaching session:

- attachment to being seen in a particular way, e.g., an expert, somebody with years of experience and knowledge, superior, valuable, 'all together' in our work and lives, never having challenges or issues, or distant and aloof;
- not sharing anything with the client about ourselves;
- trying to cover up when we feel lost in the session or off track;
- not listening deeply;

- giving advice and thinking we have all the answers;

- getting uncomfortable when a client expresses strong emotions and asking questions to distract the client from feeling what is happening for them;

- bringing the conversation back up to surface level practicalities when it gets too deep or there is too much uncertainty about where the conversation is going;

- thinking we need to be counsellors to discuss underlying issues with the client, so we avoid going into any of the underlying elements;

- asking a leading question that distracts the client from a strong emotion, from delving more deeply into what is happening for them in the moment, or at an underlying level;

- disconnecting when the client starts talking about something that is also an issue for us;

- being attached to structure, assessments, and tools as a way to ensure some sense of certainty within the coaching session;

- being attached to an outcome or getting the client to a particular point of insight in the conversation;

- trying to control the session and focusing on fixing the client;

- getting distracted by our thoughts and missing what our clients are saying;

- trying to push past any resistance from the client instead of acknowledging the resistance; and

- trying to push the client to get motivated instead of acknowledging the lack of motivation and working with what is present.

If we are aware of when we have disconnected, we can connect back with ourselves, the client, and the conversation. For example, a coach I was recently mentoring noticed that part way through the conversation, she was distracted and hadn't been listening to what the client had been saying.

The client was going into the drama and story of the situation, and the coach had gotten bored and disconnected without realising it. However, after a minute or two, she noticed she had disconnected and realised the client wasn't present either. She then asked a question that connected the client with her current, present moment experience regarding the situation, and this allowed both coach and client to connect more deeply.

When we have an agenda about where the conversation should go and direct the conversation, the client can lose their connection with themselves because they're trying to go in your direction, rather than following their internal connections. By shifting into a connection with ourselves, we can support the client to connect with themselves and go deeper to explore the underlying dynamics.

REFLECTION: Noticing and Going Deeper

Reflection What have you noticed you do to avoid connecting more deeply with your internal world? What do you do to avoid going deeper in a coaching session? Is there any other way you protect yourself? How can you support yourself to connect more deeply with self, the client, and the relationship?

Holding the Space

Holding the space means being able to sit with your client in presence, and 'hold the space' for whatever arises.

You're holding the space for thoughts, feelings, beliefs, perceptions, the client's true self, personality, inner judge, behaviours, potential, positive and negative aspects, and everything else that arises in a session. Your role is to hold your space, so you don't interfere with the client by interjecting your agenda.

When you accept that whatever arises is perfect and listen deeply enough, you will pick up key nuances in the conversation that support the client to become more aware. It's about not rejecting or judging anything.

Keys to Holding the Space

- Hold the space for yourself first. Make sure you have supported yourself to be fully present and in the moment with the client.

- Notice your judgments, attachments, and agendas. Be aware of how this gets in the way of holding the space.

- Allow the client to fully express themselves. This includes holding the space for emotions, fears, anger, drama, and whatever else arises in the space.

- Trust the holding space. Trust that by holding the space the session will progress in a way that best serves the client.

- Support your client to connect with their inner knowing. Trust that they have the inner resources to understand how to move forward in any situation.

- Acknowledge when you can't hold the space for the client. Either let the client know, refer the client to someone else, or postpone the session.

- Schedule your clients for when it is easier for you to hold the space. If, at the end of a long day, you don't have the holding space for clients, then don't schedule them at that time.

- Start the session with a mindfulness practice. This will allow you both to quiet the noisy mind and for you to hold the space in the session.

- Let others hold the space for you. To be able to hold the space we need to allow others to hold the space when we need it. This means allowing ourselves to be vulnerable enough to be supported in this way.

- Develop compassion for yourself and others. By connecting more deeply with ourselves, we naturally develop compassion for ourselves and others. It is our disconnection that leads to judgment and lack of compassion, so support yourself to stay connected and allow this compassion to naturally arise.

Another key to holding the space is supporting yourself to be grounded in the body. The more time you can spend connecting with your body through mindfulness practice and physical activity like exercise, yoga, walking, or connecting with nature, the more you will be able to hold the space. Often we get so caught up in spending most of our day in mental activity. To hold the space effectively, we need to be able to bring more attention to our body.

The analogy I often use to reflect this need for grounding is the Russian dolls that have a large base and smaller upper body. When you knock them, they don't fall over because the base is large. If you're grounded, you're not easily knocked out of your centre. However, if you're not grounded, and all your focus is on mental activity, you will be easily knocked out of your centre and thus be unable to hold the space.

Holding the Space for Emotions

Often when it comes to strong emotions, it may be difficult for coaches to stay centred and mindful. Instead, we subtly become enmeshed and over-powered by these emotions. For example, a client that is stuck and unable to figure out a way forward towards her goals might be feeling frustration or irritation. If these emotions are strong, then our holding space starts to weaken, and we will quickly start to feel similar emotions. We might then jump into reacting by trying to give her advice or a solution for how to move forward. Instead, what would have been more effective is strengthening our ability to hold ourselves in a calm and centred space, rather than being enmeshed with the client's emotions. We can then respond from this mindful space.

Coaches will often avoid going into the emotional realm of the client, thinking this is the domain of counselling. However, sometimes these emotions need to be addressed so that the client can move forward. Coaches may be concerned that if they ask the client to tap into how they are feeling, then this will make the client even more emotional. Instead, I have noticed that this rarely happens, and if it does, it is temporary. The emotion tends to disappear quickly once it is acknowledged, and then the client can think more clearly.

I recently had a client who arrived for her session, clearly holding onto some strong emotions. As she talked, I listened carefully to what was below the surface. I could hear she was trying to suppress the emotions that kept bubbling to the surface with comments such as, "I feel so silly to be getting upset," or talking about the goals she had been working on for the coaching. It was clear to me that we weren't going to move forward while these emotions continued to bubble just below the surface. I invited her to be present to her experience as she talked about this issue. I asked, 'How are feeling in this moment?' and 'What is present for you as you talk about this issue?' By supporting the client to tap into her emotions and present moment experience, rather than the story or dialogue in her head, she was able to calm down and think more clearly.

Our Emotional World

Often coaches avoid the emotional realm of coaching sessions because they are uncomfortable or disconnected from their own emotions. I have seen this for myself over the years of coaching. At first, I was very uncomfortable with emotional expression, however, as I started to explore and connect with my emotions more, it became easier for me to hold the space for others to express their emotions.

Many of us are unaware of the sadness, anger, and grief that sits below the surface of our awareness. We have suppressed these emotions for such a long time that we have no idea what it feels like to be sad or angry. We need to make space, with the use of mindfulness, to let emotions arise, to acknowledge and see them, and be with the bodily sensations that arise when we feel the emotion. Often emotions are built up through the story of what has happened. Mindfulness can help us stop identifying with the story.

By suppressing more uncomfortable emotions, we also suppress the other end of the spectrum, like joy, playfulness, compassion, and aliveness. I recently heard a story about a child who asked the question, 'Why are adults so dead inside?' Children are so full of aliveness, energy, joy, and compassion. As adults, we have lost our connection with many of these pleasant emotions. You may also notice that children are okay with expressing their sadness, anger, grief, and pain, until they are conditioned, like most adults, to suppress these emotions. To feel the joy and aliveness, we need to be willing to embrace the more uncomfortable emotions.

By becoming more aware of these emotions as coaches, we can feel more comfortable when others express strong emotions. We can stay present and avoid reacting from our aroused limbic system. We are less likely to skip over what is happening in the present moment or try to push the client to solutions. This allows the client to discover something new, creating awareness that can ultimately transform the situation and lead to insights that move them forward.

PRACTICE: Mindful Moment

Take a moment to practice mindfulness. Focus on your breath, your body, and your senses. Notice how you feel in this moment, the surrounding sounds, and the colours and textures of the surrounding objects. Bring acceptance to all that is within and around you.

Relationship Dynamics

To connect deeply, we also need to be aware of the relationship dynamics with our clients. Sometimes we can set up unhealthy relationships with others in our personal or work life, based on past experiences. Coaching relationships are no different. It is important to connect with the type of relationship you're creating with the client, ensuring that the relationship is empowering for both parties and that you're coming from a centred, mindful, and aware place in the coaching conversation.

By being mindfully aware we can notice when we project our hopes, desires, or issues onto our clients. We could be unconsciously trying to control the client by trying to fix and change them, making unfounded assumptions, or influencing them in a particular direction.

Often clients will show up in coaching with the same issues as we're dealing with in our lives. Sometimes we are aware we are dealing with these issues, and sometimes we may be unaware. Just like any relationship, the coaching relationship can be a mirror of our internal dynamics. So we can differentiate between our unresolved issues and the clients, it is particularly important to obtain the clarity of distance through mindfulness.

As a coach, you might notice you attract certain clients that represent different aspects of yourself, particularly parts you don't like and try to avoid or fix. You could be projecting these disowned aspects of yourself onto the client. For example, if you attract clients that feel disempowered and victimised, you may try unsuccessfully to fix them, and feel defeated because they aren't making any progress. It is possible that you're projecting your internal victim or disempowerment onto this client.

By acknowledging, being aware of, and mindfully experiencing this aspect of yourself, you will find a more empowering way of working with these clients.

It is important to have empathy and compassion, and trust that this person is exactly where they need to be, that there is nothing to fix or change. Instead, your job is to uncover what is already there. When you come from this space of mindfulness, noticing your projections and being able to respond rather than react, the connection between coach and client deepens.

REFLECTION: Noticing Projections

Who are you being with the client? What aspects of yourself do you need to own more? What might you be projecting onto your clients?

Underlying Energy in a Conversation

To create a mindful connection with the client, it can be useful to feel the underlying energy in a session. Often you may not become aware of this until after the session, so making some space afterwards to reflect on what was happening in the session can be useful.

For example, I was being coached recently, and throughout the session, I was in a calm, relaxed, and reflective state. There was a little 'aha' moment which created energy, but for the most part, I was content to simply explore and reflect. However, at one point I could feel the coach was going into a high-energy state. She asked questions like, 'What would it feel like to feel fantastic in this area?' or 'What would get you excited?' And she did it with excitement in her voice. However, I wasn't feeling excited. The coach had an agenda to push me into feeling excited, so I would feel motivated to take action. I was happy being in the reflective mode until the insight occurred and the motivation arose naturally.

As a result, the coach was in a different space, energetically. I noticed this created some distance in the session as I started to retreat energetically from the coach. After we debriefed, the coach acknowledged she had been attached to getting me into a space of feeling excited, and that she had become anxious (limbic) because I didn't seem to be moving toward my goals. She measured her success as a coach on whether I had an insight, felt excited, and ready to move into action. Her strategy to deal with this was to create the energy for me, but this had the opposite effect. The connection between us was lost in that moment, and this need to push the energy was exhausting for the coach.

Often we feel it is our responsibility to make the client feel better, excited and energised, and we need to do that through our energy. However, it can have the opposite effect if the client is in a different energy space. We need to bring mindful awareness to where the client is, rather than trying to push them to be somewhere they aren't ready to go to yet. Through this mindful acceptance, we can pick up on the energy, the subtle signals of the conversation, and ask questions that will lead to a new awareness.

• CHAPTER 4 •

COMMUNICATING WITH MINDFULNESS

Communicating with Mindfulness

When we have established a strong base of presence in the coaching session, communicating becomes natural, spontaneous, and in the flow of the conversation. The coach is open, accepting, non-judgmental, and able to hold the space for the client. 'Who' the coach is being is conveyed through her energy and the client feels this energy from the coach.

As coaches, we communicate with more than just words. We communicate with our tone of voice, body language, the particular words we use, the words we emphasise, the way we hesitate, how we use silence, and a multitude of other ways we communicate through our energy. It is the non-verbal communication that speaks the loudest when we communicate with clients. Mindfulness supports us to be aware of what we're communicating energetically.

Intuitively, often without realising it, our clients pick up on our energy as soon as they see or hear us. Our brains are hardwired to pick up subtle messages through body language, including tone of voice and the way we speak. As humans, we often think we can hide what we are feeling or thinking. However, it shows up subtly in our energy field. Even if the client can't articulate what they're sensing, they can feel what you're energetically transmitting.

On a more obvious level, a client will sense if your mind is busy and distracted or if you're rushing or pushing them to get to an outcome. This often sets up a subtle form of resistance from the client, without them even realising they're resisting. If you have an agenda about how your client should move forward, or what they should do, they will sense this at a subtle level.

Alternatively, if you show up for the session calm and having practiced mindfulness, your mind will be clear and peaceful. The client will feel this from you and, as a result, will often start relaxing and feeling more like they can trust you. Their thoughts will be clearer, and they will have deeper, more profound insights because their limbic system will have dampened enough to allow the prefrontal region to create new awareness.

Automatic Habits of Communicating

As coaches, it can be useful to notice our communication habits and the impact these habits have on the coaching relationship. Some of these habits will be useful for supporting the client, but others will not be as supportive to the client.

Consider:

Do you interrupt while the client is speaking?

- Do you wait for an answer when you ask permission, or do you jump in before the client responds with a yes or no?
- Is your pace too fast?

- Do you jump in to fill the silence?

- Do you subtly communicate with your energy that you're the expert?

- Do you say 'yeah' or 'okay' or just move onto another question based on your agenda after a client has shared?

- Is your body language closed and contracted or open and light?

- Is your tone of voice light or heavy?

- Do you say 'um' or 'okay' or other repetitive words to fill the space?

- Do you use too many words to fill the space?

- Are you thinking about the next question when you listen to the client, thus communicating that you're not listening?

Noticing our automatic habits of communication isn't about being self-conscious, but instead, it is about being mindful of how effective we are in communicating.

It's also about bringing mindfulness to habits and looking at the intention, emotions, bodily sensations, and thoughts behind these habits. For example, if you prefer to talk rather than allow silence in a conversation, then look at what the root of this is for you. Perhaps silence makes you uncomfortable. Notice the discomfort when it arises, be curious about this habit and what arises when you're talking instead of allowing silence.

For example, I was mentoring a coach who kept interrupting the client before he had finished speaking and maintained a fast pace during the session. It wasn't enough for the coach to start a new habit of not interrupting and slowing down the pace; she needed to be more mindful of what was behind the habit.

This coach noticed she would feel anxious, her heart felt as if it contracted, and she had thoughts questioning the value she offered in the session. She maintained a fast pace of speaking because she felt that the more she fit into the session, the more the client would get from the session. She also wanted the client to experience her as an expert and valuable resource, so she interrupted to demonstrate this value.

She became mindfully aware that she did this in other areas of her life, like with her children and husband, and was going through her life at a fast pace. When she slowed down to experience what was happening for her in the moment, she noticed tension in her chest, anxiety, and the thought, 'If I don't provide value, then I'm worthless.' Her insight was that she associated her worth with giving value to others. These thoughts, feelings and body sensations were driving her behaviour in the session.

In this situation, mindful awareness was critical. When she was mindfully aware of what was happening at a deep level, she was able to slow down, leave more silence, and not interrupt the client. She was able to notice when these thoughts, feelings, and sensations arose in the session, and she was able to stay with the client, rather than be hijacked by her experience.

REFLECTION: Noticing Habits

What communication habits have you developed? These can either be verbal or non-verbal. What is the impact of these habits? What do you notice about your body sensations, feelings and thoughts, when you're communicating in this way?

One way to identify habits is to record a coaching session and listen back to the recording to identify how you communicated in the session.

Some tips for communicating powerfully with mindfulness are:

- use as few words as possible to communicate - the more succinct and specific your communication, the more likely you will be understood;

- avoid asking double or triple questions - often the best questions are simple and clear;

- be direct when communicating - if you don't know how to express something, try being direct rather than using too many words to explain;

- when you ask permission, make sure you wait for a 'yes' or 'no' response;

- use silence to communicate your trust in the client to develop ideas, thoughts, and solutions;

- maintain your presence when in the silence, holding the space rather than thinking about the next question or comment;

- slow down the pace so you can communicate clearly, notice if you tend to rush when you communicate as this is often a sign that your mind is racing ahead, rather than being present as you communicate;

- allow yourself to pause before you speak, taking a moment to pause allows you to take in what has just been communicated by the client before formulating your next question or comment; and

- when you notice you have been distracted or if you feel lost in the coaching conversation, it's always useful to recap the main points in the conversation to check that you're both aligned before moving forward.

REFLECTION: Developing New Habits

What habits would you like to develop when communicating with your clients? Identify at least one habit and focus on practicing in the next week with your clients.

Mindful Listening

Listening with mindfulness means being present when you're listening. Often we listen for the next powerful question to ask or the next comment to propel the client toward insight and moving forward. Alternately, we might have some unconscious dialogue going in the background about the value of what we are offering, the limited time we have for the session, and whether we are 'enough' for this client. As a result, we're distracted while we're listening.

By practicing mindfulness, we train our mind to be in the moment with the client. We trust that by listening deeply, we will intuitively know what the next question or clarification needs to be in the moment, rather than before the moment.

Acceptance and Non-judgment

Mindful listening is listening from a place of acceptance and non-judgment. In other words, accepting without judgment everything that arises in the conversation, or at the very least, noticing our judgment and ensuring it doesn't get in the way of the connection with the client.

It is important we see that our judgments are about ourselves, rather than about the client. For example, if we judge the client for not making more progress, even on a very subtle level, this is perhaps our fear that they won't get the results they want from the coaching, meaning we have made ourselves responsible for the client's results. To listen deeply, we need to loosen our identification with these judgments, which are simply thoughts we keep thinking and identifying with. If we can notice the judgment in the background, we can move our attention away from it and instead, focus on listening more deeply to the client to support them to create new awareness.

We want to bring mindfulness to every part of what the client is communicating, even those parts of the conversation that might seem irrelevant to the topic the client is discussing. Sometimes, the client might even dismiss something they're saying as not relevant, however, if you support the client to explore the links to the topic, it becomes apparent that what they're saying is very relevant and often pivotal to a shift in perspective for the client.

For example, a client came into the session talking about an argument she had with her husband, which didn't seem relevant to the goals she had set about improving her ability to lead an effective team. However, after asking a few questions, she realised the argument was about her lack of commitment to the relationship, which was also the issue with her team. She discovered that she had been holding back from being fully committed to her team, always looking for a better job offer, and thus sabotaging any opportunity to create an effective, inspired, committed team.

To mindfully listen, we also need to be aware of our attachment to a perspective that might be different to the clients. We need to avoid coming across as judgmental of the client's current perspective and assuming our point of view is the 'right' one. For example, I had a client recently who talked about how in all of his relationships the other person seemed to be lacking in awareness, and this is why he had to end the relationships. I have a slightly different view of relationships. I see relationships as a mirror of our internal world. Although this perspective might have been a useful perspective for the client, I needed to be aware of my judgments and remain open to his perspective on the situation.

I focused on listening and supporting the client to get to this new perspective himself if that was what was needed in the conversation. Of course, there might be some other way he needed to shift his perspective that would be more powerful, and something he was more ready to see, rather than what I thought was 'right'.

Listening to the Client's Connections

Mindful listening is about noticing the client's connections, rather than trying to fit what the client is saying into our frame of mind or context so we can make connections or have insights. In the above example, if I'm listening to the client for how I can fit what he is saying into how I see relationships, then I'm not listening deeply. Instead, I'm listening to what my mind is saying and how it wants to interpret it. Sometimes, offering what you're seeing is useful in the coaching. However, it can also be an attempt to steer the client in a particular direction, rather than listening deeply and supporting the client to make their connections.

Listening to the Whole Being

When we listen with mindfulness, we are also listening to the whole being, rather than fixating on a particular aspect. We can tune into the big picture of the client and who the client is as a whole, rather than as a list of certain qualities. For example, we might have a goal of supporting the client to fix a behaviour, like cultivating better relationships by listening rather than interrupting, however, we see the client as more than this one issue. We see all the client's multifaceted parts, as well as who they are at a deeper level. We can see this behaviour as a symptom, rather than something that defines the client.

How it Feels to Mindfully Listen

When we listen mindfully, we're relaxed, centred, and content to allow the conversation to unfold. We're able to notice and be curious about different elements of the conversation. There is a lightness to the coaching that allows space for reflection and insight.

On the other hand, when we listen without mindfulness, the conversation can be confusing and go around in circles. You and the client might feel agitated, stuck, or sense that something is missing, like something else might have been possible in this coaching conversation. If you notice this happening, then see it as an indication you need to be more mindful, listen deeply and open to new possibilities in the conversation.

Practice is the Key

The key to mindful listening is to practice mindfulness, both formally in sitting practice, and informally in everyday life. The more you embed these connections for mindfulness in the brain, the more likely you will have a deep presence when coaching.

A particularly informative place to practice mindfulness is with those individuals who you find it difficult to listen to attentively. The next time you have a conversation with this person, use the time to practice being mindfully present and notice what distracts you. Usually, these are the same things that subtly distract you in other areas; it's not just about this person. Notice how you can support yourself to be mindful in these conversations.

PRACTICE: Mindful Listening

Find a comfortable, quiet space to sit for 10 minutes. Start by focusing on your breathing, closing your eyes, and feeling your body. Notice how you feel in this moment. Take a few deep breaths if needed and then support the mind to quiet by bringing your focus to the surrounding sounds.

Notice the obvious sounds around you and then notice those that are less obvious. There is no need to label, fixate, or stay with a sound. Instead, move your attention from sound to sound.

Imagine your ears being as large as possible and picking up on all the sounds in your environment. There is no need to stretch or strain to hear anything, just simply allow your attention to move freely.

Try to notice the faintest sound in your environment.

Perhaps, also, notice silence and what that sounds like.

Spend at least 5 to 10 minutes just noticing the surrounding sounds. When you notice your attention being distracted by thoughts, gently bring your attention back to noticing the surrounding sounds.

Then bring your awareness back to the body, breath, and open your eyes.

You can also do this exercise in everyday life, while you're walking down the street, driving a car (with eyes open, of course), on public transport, washing the dishes, etc. Try this exercise while listening to music. Pay careful attention to the different tones and changes in the music.

Whatever you notice during this exercise, there's a good chance they're common habits you experience on a regular basis. In everyday life, when everything moves at a fast pace, it's difficult to be mindful and spot these habits. We go into default mode easily when listening. By becoming more aware of them with this exercise, you open up the possibility of noticing them in real-time in a coaching session. Then you can start to change those habits that affect the listening.

Listening Beyond the Words

Mindful listening is about listening for the information available in the moment, and not just what the client is saying. The words are a fraction of what is being said. The rest is said through body language, energy, emotion, and tone of voice. We need to develop mindfulness to pick up on more of this information.

Words

Although words are a fraction of what is being said, they are still very important. It can be particularly useful to reflect back to the client if they use a word repetitively to see if this means anything for the client. You can also reflect back that they emphasised a particular word and check to see if this is important to the conversation.

It can also be useful to support the client to explore the deeper meaning of a word. For example, a client uses the word 'conscious' about the type of relationships they want to have with others. You could explore this with the client by saying, 'You used the word conscious to describe the type of relationship you want to have with others, what does this mean for you?' I might have an understanding of what I mean by the word conscious. However, this might be entirely different from what the client means. Also, the client may not have thought about what the word means for them, so it supports them to gain a deeper understanding.

Tone of Voice

The tone someone uses when speaking is full of information. Often it is useful to establish a baseline for the tone the client uses. This is usually obvious after one or two sessions, and then you may start to notice when the client varies from this tone. Notice when the client raises their tone when talking about particular topics and when they lower their tone on other topics.

We express emotion through our tone of voice. When excited, our tone might pick up and be filled with energy. When sad or resigned, we might lower our tone of voice and speak heavily. When we are calm and relaxed, we might speak slowly and with lightness.

The pace of speaking also indicates how present the client is in the session. Often I notice that when a client is speaking quickly and hardly stopping to take a breath, it is likely their mind is very active, and their feeling anxious, fearful, or some other related emotion.

It is important to remember that as coaches, we are simply there to reflect back what we hear and see, instead of making assumptions about what we hear. For example, if you heard the client's tone of voice increase in volume while talking about a relationship, you might conclude that they're excited about the situation,. However, they may be experiencing something completely different. So instead of saying 'you must be excited about this new relationship,' you could say, 'I noticed your tone of voice increased in energy, what was happening for in that moment?' In other words, it isn't up to us to conclude what the tone or pace of the voice means. Instead, allows the client to explore what this means, as well as supporting them to be present to their experience.

Body Language

As humans, we're constantly reading body language, whether conscious or unconscious. By developing mindfulness in coaching, we're consciously able to pick up on more of this information.

Our bodies constantly give off signals that are easily decoded by our brains. While the prefrontal cortex or thinking brain might be able to lie about how we are feeling, our bodies, which are controlled by the more hard-wired parts of the brain, cannot lie. So the client might use words that contradict what the body is saying. This contradiction can be useful for us to reflect back to our clients.

There is plenty of literature on what different body language means. Although this can be useful to understand, it is more important to support the client to understand and be mindful of their body language. For example, the client might touch his heart every time he talks about a particular person, so you might reflect back what you noticed to the client. Or you might notice that a client hesitates before saying something. You might say to him, 'I noticed you hesitated before you said that. What was happening?' The client can then tune in and be mindful of what was happening for him when he hesitated.

Energy

Listening for energy variations in the conversations can also be useful. You will notice that before a client has an insight, they are in a reflective space. There might be long periods of silence and a low level of energy. The client is listening internally to subtle signals, so they need to quiet the mental chatter to listen to these signals. Then, when the insight occurs, there tends to be more energy and the client feels motivated to move forward.

You can also notice the different levels of energy, when the client is talking about different topics, ideas, or issues. For example, I had a client who wanted to find a job she enjoyed. She had a lot of energy around starting up her own business, and very little energy around going to find another job. I pointed out what I had noticed about her energy, and she had an insight that she would likely be more successful at running her own business because she had more energy for it. It became clear that she wanted to start her own business, so we worked together to find a way to put this into action.

Emotions

Supporting clients to be mindful of their emotions can be a powerful part of the coaching process. Often certain emotions are hidden from view, so reflecting back to a client when you sense an emotion can support them to shift the emotion, rather than staying stuck in it. When stuck, these emotions can prevent clients from thinking clearly and coming up with new possibilities for moving forward. When the limbic system is aroused, bringing awareness to the emotion can dampen this response so the pre-frontal thinking brain can start working again.

Summary

When listening with mindfulness, there are endless amounts of infor-
. mation on which to focus and pick up on in the conversation. You don't need to pick up on it all. The idea is to be mindful and then notice these

elements as they come into your awareness. By picking up and reflecting on what you're hearing or sensing, you will be supporting the client to create new awareness.

PRACTICE: The Mindful Listener

This mindful listening exercise will help you become more aware of how mindful you are as you listen to someone speak and what distracts you. You can do this exercise with a friend, family member, or co-worker.

Allocate 5 minutes each for the exercise. Decide who will be the speaker first and who will be the listener.

The speaker is to speak for 5 minutes without interruption by the listener. It doesn't matter what the topic is; you can try changing to a few different topics. Just speak about whatever comes to mind. If you run out of things to say, just stop speaking and sit in silence until you feel like talking again. Your turn is over when 5 minutes is up.

While the speaker is speaking, the listener focuses on listening with mindfulness. Notice your inner dialogue as the speaker is talking. Resist the urge to say anything or interrupt. As you're listening, notice the following:

- What emotions are you experiencing?

- Do you feel the urge to give advice?

- What assumptions are you making about the speaker and the topic?

- What are the unspoken qualities in the interaction?

- Do you feel the urge to share your story?

- What other thoughts are distracting you?

- Are you feeling the urge to rescue or make the other person feel better?

Write down your insights from this exercise and reflect on how you can support yourself to be more mindful in your listening with others.

———————————————————

• CHAPTER 5 •

MINDFULNESS
AND INTUITION

Defining Intuition

Mindfulness is about being fully awake in our lives. It is about perceiving the exquisite vividness of each moment. We also gain immediate access to our own powerful inner resources for insight, transformation, and healing.

–Jon Kabat-Zinn, *Mindfulness for Beginners.*

Intuition is often described as a 'hunch', a 'gut feeling' or 'something my heart is telling me'. It is a feeling about something you can't explain. It seems illogical and irrational. However, there is some feeling that what you're sensing is right, even though your mind can't explain it.

Here are some definitions of intuition:

Carl Jung defined intuition as 'perception via the unconscious' to bring forth ideas, images, possibilities, and ways out of a blocked situation.

American Heritage Dictionary: 'The act or faculty of knowing or sensing without the use of rational processes; immediate cognition; perceptive insight.'

Roget's Thesaurus: 'Intuitive cognition: feeling, hunch, idea, impression, suspicion. The power to discern the true nature of a person or situation; insight, instinct, etc.'

Robert Graves: 'Intuition is the supra-logic that cuts out all the routine processes of thought and leaps'.

Debunking Myths about Intuition

There are many myths about intuition that tend to get in the way of using this skill effectively. We shut down our ability to sense intuition because of the beliefs we have about what it is and what it can do.

Here are some common myths:

Myth #1: You have to be born with intuitive ability.

While some seem to have a greater level of skill in this area, the reality is that we are all born intuitive. We can all learn to develop the skill just like anything else we focus on learning.

Myth #2: You have to wait for intuition to hit you

Intuition is always available. However, we often ignore it until we get a flash of intuitive insight, which makes it feel as if it has come from out of nowhere. The reality is that in that particular moment we didn't have filters preventing us from connecting to the subtle signals of intuition.

Myth #3: Intuition works the same way for everyone.

How we connect and listen to intuition is different for everyone. We all have our own way of sensing intuition. Some individuals see images, and others hear words or a voice. We might feel an emotion or bodily sensation, or a combination of these different forms of sensing intuition.

Myth #4: Only women are intuitive.

It is true that women seem to have wiring that tends towards connecting with intuition. One likely reason for this is that our tribal, female ancestors were more in tune with the tribe, the relationships, and making sure all was harmonious. Their intuition about others was heightened as a result. However, intuition isn't just a female trait; both men and women regularly use intuition throughout each day.

Myth #5: Having intuition means you can predict the future, or you can read minds.

Intuition isn't about seeing the future or being psychic. Being psychic is a highly developed form of intuition and focused in a particular direction, like mind reading or predicting the future. Intuition is more about sensing what is here in this moment.

Myth #6: There is no rational way to explain intuition, therefore, it isn't credible.

Just because the rational mind can't explain something doesn't mean there is not a logical explanation. For example, you might have a feeling of fear in your stomach as your client arrives for a session and have no idea why. She starts the session by telling you about a traumatic experience she has been through in the past week and the fear that this has brought up for her.

Myth #7: Intuition is foolproof.

Intuition isn't foolproof. At times, trusting our intuition means going in a direction that might lead us to a place we didn't want to go. For example, having the intuition to take on a new client only to have the client turn out to be a significant challenge, often arriving late and not doing the work or taking ownership. This unwanted result could mean that we didn't accurately pick up on our intuition or perhaps choose to take on this client so we could see something about ourselves.

Myth #8: Intuition has no practical application.

There are a lot of ways we use intuition every day. For example, to make decisions about who to hire, whether to take that job, to go on that date with someone or how to go about expanding a business.

Myth #9: Intuitive people are illogical (flaky, lacking intelligence).

Since intuitive decisions, hunches, or ideas don't seem to make sense, it might seem illogical to others. Our society focuses a lot of energy on rationality and certainty, whereas intuition depends on relaxing into uncertainty and trusting what you're sensing.

Myth #10: If intuition doesn't work once, then we should drop it and be more logical.

Often people give up trying to trust their intuition because they trust what they think is intuition and it turns out to be incorrect, so they decide it isn't worth trusting their intuition. It is unreasonable to expect that intuition will always be correct or that you will always have interpreted the intuition correctly. A part of learning to trust intuition is a process of trial and error. This is how you learn what is and isn't intuition, as well as how to accurately interpret what you pick up on.

REFLECTION: Exploring Intuition

What are some of your common beliefs about intuition? Perhaps it is the messages you have received from others about intuition. How do these beliefs interfere with your ability to sense intuition?

Science of intuition

The basis of intuition is in nonverbal communication and that our brains, as masters of pattern recognition, can sense very quickly when something is out of sequence.

- Jonah Lehrer, *The Decisive Moment.*

Intuition is a tricky topic to study and measure. However, there are a few areas of research that indicate what might be happening when we use intuition.

One useful part of the research explains that the basis of intuition is the retrieval of implicit memories or connections that have been encoded in our unconscious or hardwired through past experience.[13] Our brains scan our environment using the senses to look for patterns and identify anything that is out of sequence. We often go through this process long before our conscious minds have caught up with what we have unconsciously processed.

For example, studies done with nurses in the 1980s found that those nurses who had been in the profession for a long time saw and made better

---

13 http://scienceblogs.com/neurophilosophy/2009/02/09/the-neurological-basis-of-intuition/

judgments more quickly. This ability was referred to as intuition.[14] It is assumed that the nurses, through their past experience, had hardwired the information into their unconscious. They were then able to draw on these implicit connections to make the assessment of the patient's situation or make decisions quickly.

One way this ability to pick up on unconscious hardwiring is most relevant for coaching is with body language, including facial expressions, tone of voice, and body movements. Our brains are expert decoders of body language. These signals are easily noticed by the receiver. However, it is harder for the sender to suppress them, which often gives away a lot of information without the sender realising it.

For example, assume you sense that someone is upset, even though he says he is fine. It is your intuition telling you that something is amiss, and your brain has possibly picked up something about his facial expressions, body language, tone of voice, or some other non-verbal cue, and computed a mismatch with the verbal message, and you receive a strong message that something is wrong.

Have you ever heard the expression 's/he smiles with his/her eyes'? This expression is often used as a way to describe someone who is happy, genuine, and trustworthy. When someone smiles and is genuinely happy to see another person, the muscles around the eyes contract involuntarily. If the smile is more reluctant, unsure, or shy, the eye muscles don't move, and we might unconsciously conclude that the person's 'smile didn't reach their eyes', that they're hiding something, or being fake. We unconsciously pick up these subtle clues from the other person's body language.

There is also research indicating that we have a large network of neural pathways in the heart and stomach that communicate with the brain about what they are sensing. We often say we have a 'gut feel' or our 'heart tells us this is right', which articulates what happens as we physically sense in the belly and the heart.

---

14 Linköping University. *Intuition Can Be Explained.* ScienceDaily

It is useful to develop a deeper connection with the belly and the heart during mindfulness practice, by sensing the bodily sensations in these parts of the body. You can also take it a step further and sense what these parts might be telling you or what feelings are connected to the bodily sensations.

Intuition and Insight

Intuition and insight are often seen as the same, but there are slight differences. Insight is a sense of clarity, the 'aha!' moment where everything makes sense and becomes clear, and there is a sense of certainty and understanding.

On the other hand, intuition is a sense or gut feeling about a direction or a path to be followed, quite often without knowing the reason for going in that direction.

When insight occurs the logic of the solution, that's been arrived at suddenly becomes crystal clear and can be explained, in words, numbers or an image. Intuition, on the other hand, creates a sense (a gut feeling or hunch) of a direction to be followed (a signpost) or of an impending solution (a feeling of knowing).

–Eugene Sadler-Smith, *The Intuitive Mind.*

I have noticed that intuition often comes just before insight. By giving the client some space to reflect and quiet the mind chatter, they become more in tune with what is emerging for them. If we are also in tune, we can support them to go in the direction of that hunch. By exploring these subtle connections the client can often get to a moment of insight where all the pieces fit together.

What we sense intuitively can sometimes be hard to explain in words and perhaps might even seem irrational, however, as a coach, by acting from intuition and supporting your client to tune into intuition, you're supporting them to have new insights and gain new levels of awareness.

Speaking from your intuition is extraordinarily valuable in coaching. It is right up there with the ability to listen deeply and deftly. Yet even though we can define it in words, the experience of intuition is sometimes hard to explain, which also makes it difficult for some people to accept. For many people, the trouble starts with the difficulty of verifying intuition. Sometimes there's no observable evidence for the conclusion. In some cases, the conclusions people derive from their intuition are actually contrary to observable evidence.

Henry Kimsey-House & Karen Kimsey-House,

Co-Active Coaching

PRACTICE: Mindful Moment

Take a moment to practice mindfulness. Focus on your breath, your body, and your senses. Notice how you feel in this moment, the surrounding sounds, and the colours and textures of the surrounding objects. Bring acceptance to all that is within and around you.

Connecting with Intuition

Many people sense their intuition in their bodies, for example, in their chests or stomachs. Some feel goose bumps all over their bodies or a tingling in their fingers. For others, it might be an image, a word or sound.

Take some time to find out how you sense intuition. Stop, pay attention, and tune into your senses to determine how the communication shows up.

Here are some common indicators of intuition:

Physical sensations. For example, heaviness, lightness, chills, restlessness, physical pain, discomfort in the belly, goosebumps, a spinning sensation, spontaneous tears, warmth in hands or base of the spine, tightness in the chest.

Feelings. For example, uneasiness, concern, confusion, joy, euphoria, a profound peace, clarity, a sense of assuredness, or something feeling 'right'.

Sounds, words, or visual images that indicate or give information about a situation or person.

Other senses: smell, touch, taste. These are more uncommon than ones listed above.

One of the interesting things about intuition is its elusive quality. Looking too intently for it makes it more difficult to find. If you are working too hard to find your intuition, your attention is on you and your efforts. By shifting your attention to the question or the other person and opening the channel, you can more easily find the answer. The key seems to be to take a soft focus, be open. Your intuition is there, giving you messages or clues, just below the surface. This is the paradox of intuition: an open hand will hold it; it will slip through a fist.

–Henry Kimsey-House & Karen Kimsey-House, *Co-Active Coaching.*

REFLECTION: Listening to Subtle Signals

Think of a time when you just knew something. It could be in your work, coaching, or personal life.

Describe the situation. What did you notice was different in this situation (i.e., about yourself, another person, the situation, etc.)? How did you feel? What sensations did you notice in your body? Was there anything else you noticed about your intuition in this situation?

Blocks to Intuition

Since the signals from intuition are so subtle, it is often difficult to tune into intuition and understand what it is communicating with us. We have many blocks or challenges that often prevent us from tuning in. To support ourselves to access intuition, we need to be aware of the blocks as they arise.

Strong emotions

When there is a strong emotion or the limbic system is aroused it is much harder to be 'in tune' in a coaching session. When the limbic system is aroused, it is possible to do things instinctively, to support us in emergencies to move into a fight, flight, or freeze mode. In a coaching session, however, this isn't necessarily useful, as this limbic system response can cause confusion and the inability to pick up on subtle signals. Even if we can sense intuition, we often don't interpret it correctly because our prefrontal brain is reduced in capacity.

We need to ensure our limbic systems are dampened down so we can listen to subtle signals. To do this, we need to be aware of strong emotional triggers and practice mindfulness to dampen down the response.

Our hardwired perception

Our hardwiring might support us to unconsciously pick up on intuition, such as the earlier example with the nurses. However, it can also block us from accurately picking up on what we sense intuitively.

We may think we're tuning into intuition. However, we are relying on our embedded perceptions, beliefs, and knowledge, instead, which may or may not be correct. For example, after working with a client for a while, it is easy for us to assume certain things about the client and how to approach the coaching session. These assumptions may limit the possibility of something new arising from the conversation. Intuition is being crowded out by the perceptions and the need to maintain these perceptions as a way of ensuring certainty.

The other trap is that we notice our intuition and misinterpret it through the filter of our hardwiring. For example, if you pick up on the client hesitating, and intuitively sense it important to inquire into what caused this hesitation, you might ask, 'I noticed you hesitated; what was happening for you?' without needing to label what was happening for the client. If we filter it through our hardwiring, however, we may interpret the client's hesitation as being reluctant to share and not trusting you in the coaching session. You might fall into self-criticism and become distracted from listening when in reality, the client hesitated because she wanted to say what she felt without needing to filter it. So it is important not to make assumptions about what you sense. Instead, share what you're sensing and let the client determine its importance and relevance.

Distractions

We live in a society that thrives on distractions; we are constantly bombarded with information and our minds become very noisy. We get distracted easily, and too much neural activity can distract us from listening to the very subtle signals of intuition, so it is important to quiet the neural activity of the mind.

Mindfulness is the primary tool that supports you to quiet the mind. However, it is also useful to look at what else might support you to reduce the amount of sensory input you receive each day. You can do this by switching off the television or spending less time on the computer, watching the news, checking emails or social media, and spending more time in nature, sitting with a cup of tea, writing in a journal, gardening, or whatever else supports you to quiet down the mind chatter.

By taking the time to quiet the mind, you will enter a session with a client with a quiet mind, rather than letting the noise distract you from listening to your intuition and the client.

Also, it is important to deal with any external distractions in the session, ensuring the session takes place in a quiet, safe space, that the client is comfortable and has what they need to feel open and reflective in the session.

Tuning in and Trusting Intuition

The process for 'tuning in' is to develop the skill of mindfulness. Mindfulness can dampen the limbic system if it is aroused. It also makes us more aware of the hardwiring that might be driving our perception and brings our attention away from any distractions.

One of the most important ways of creating the conditions for intuitions to arise is through a process of quieting the analytical mind. The assumption behind this is that the voice of the intuitive mind may be drowned out by the constant verbalisations of the analytical mind.

– Eugene Sadler-Smith, *The Intuitive Mind.*

After we quiet our mind, we can easily become aware of what intuition is communicating. However, we also often quickly dismiss the intuition as being irrational, doubt the intuition, or feel it is too much of a risk to follow the intuition. Often in coaching situations, a coach will have an intuition about something that could make a big difference to the client, but she doubts what she is sensing and dismisses the intuition. Often it feels a bit too much of a risk to reveal what she is sensing.

To begin trusting your intuition, you need to act on it more. In a coaching session, it means taking a risk to share what you're sensing and checking whether it resonates with the client. Either they will confirm what you have said has resonated, or they will brush over it and move on, or let you know it doesn't feel right. You can't get it wrong provided you have given the client space to disagree with you, so they can let you know what resonates. The more you practice sharing what you're sensing, the better you will get at noticing intuition and knowing when to share it.

Using intuition in coaching isn't just about sharing an observation it might also come in the form of asking a question or using a tool with the client. Or you might intuitively feel it is time to recap or summarise the conversation and this supports the conversation to go to a deeper level.

REFLECTION: Supporting your Intuition

Pick one area of your life where you intuitively know action needs to be taken. Identify what will support you to take action and trust your intuition.

Also, identify what will support you to trust and act on intuition more in your coaching sessions.

Intuition often shows up in unexpected ways in the coaching conversation. Sometimes it's a hunch. Or it might appear as a visual image or an unexplained shift in emotion or energy. The important thing to remember in coaching is to be open to intuition. Trusting it, [being] aware of it, and completely unattached to the interpretation. In the end, intuition is valuable when it moves the client to action or deeper learning. It is irrelevant, really, whether your intuition was "correct".

–Henry Kimsey-House & Karen Kimsey-House, *Co-Active Coaching.*

PRACTICE: Mindful Moment

Take a moment to practice mindfulness. Focus on your breath, your body, and your senses. Notice how you feel in this moment, the surrounding sounds, the colours and the textures of the surrounding objects. Bring acceptance to all that is within and around you.

Communicating Intuition

We need to be mindful as coaches when we communicate something we sense intuitively, to ensure we express ourselves in a way in which the intuition can be heard, doesn't trip the limbic system, and the client feels empowered.

Checking your Intention

It is important to check where you're coming from when sharing the intuition so the client can feel empowered by what you sense. Are you coming from a place of fear or love? Are you connected to your heart when sharing?

If you're coming from a space of fear, disconnected from your heart or self, trying to get the client somewhere, or affirming yourself as the expert, this will feel disempowering for the client. Even if the intuition is correct, the client may resist hearing it because they feel like you're trying to tell them something or give advice instead of empowering them to sense what is happening for them and decide what resonates. The client might think it judgmental, rather than affirming.

I have noticed coaches who are very intuitive and accurately pick up on what is happening for the client. However, when they have little connection to their hearts, they deliver the intuition in a way that doesn't empower the client and feels judgmental, and the client ends up resisting the information on some level.

Make sure you check in and sense where you're coming from. Notice your body and how you're feeling. Is there contraction or expansion, heaviness or lightness? Do you feel connected or disconnected? Are you pushing or forcing the client to see something? Are you in the moment? If you're in a place of fear or disconnection, then it is probably best to come back to the intuition later, if necessary, and instead, focus on being with the client, connecting to yourself, and listening deeply. If the intuition shows up again, and you feel connected, then it is most likely worthwhile sharing.

Asking Permission

At times it can be useful to ask permission before sharing what you're sensing. It might go something like this: 'I would like to share something with you about what I'm picking up, is that okay? It might be right, or it may not be; just see if it resonates for you.' Also, make sure you wait for the client to confirm it is okay to share and make space for the client to say 'no' if needed. It's possible they might be connected to sensing something for themselves and your sharing at that moment might interrupt their process.

Share your process

It can also be useful to share with the client your intuitive process. Sharing your process supports the client to understand where your observation fits in within the context of the conversation. Sometimes you might pick something up, and it might be relevant, however hard for the client to accept if they don't understand where it might fit in.

For example, instead of saying, 'I'm sensing you feel under pressure in this situation,' you could say, 'I have noticed during this conversation you have been speaking quickly and taking shallow breaths. You've also mentioned a few times others high expectations of you. I'm sensing you're feeling under pressure, does this feel right to you?'

Using a Question

One of the best ways to communicate an intuition is to phrase it as a question. For example, if you had an intuition about the lack of commitment to a relationship as being an underlying issue, you could ask, 'How do you feel about commitment in this relationship?' This is an open question that allows the client space to decide if it is relevant and if they to explore it further.

Clarifying the Essence

A powerful way to communicate intuition is by clarifying the essence of what isn't being said in as few words as possible. For example, you might say, 'What I'm hearing is…' or 'What I'm picking up on is that you feel…' or 'What it sounds like is…' or 'I'm sensing that this might be…' We need to be mindful to pick up on what isn't being said verbally, however, is being said through tone of voice, body language and the client's energy.

Using Other Words

You may have a client who is comfortable with the idea of intuition, and you can say, 'Can I share what my intuition is telling me?' or 'My intuition is that you are…' However, some clients are uncomfortable with the word intuition, and you might be better off using other words, such as gut feeling or what is heart telling you.

Use the Client's Modality

When communicating intuition, it can be useful to use the client's preferred modality. For example, does the client tend to be kinaesthetic, auditory, or visual? You can then use words related to their modality in your questions. You can usually get a sense of this in the first couple of sessions by the language they use, for example, 'I feel…' or 'I think…' or 'I see…', or 'I sense…', etc.

It is useful to speak in the client's modality wherever possible. For example:

- Kinaesthetic: 'Do you feel…?'

- Visual: 'I see an image of x,' or 'Like a swimmer waiting for the starting gun,' or 'Do you see yourself as x?'

- Auditory: 'I hear that you're confused,' or 'I can hear your thoughts about this are conflicting,' or 'It's like there is too much noise in the room when this person is present.'

- Mental: 'Do you think…' or 'I think that this might be…' or 'it feels like you have made your mind up about this situation.'

Being Curious

Bring a sense of curiosity to your questions around intuition, rather than taking an all-knowing approach. For example, you could say, 'I'm just curious about the connection between this situation and your work?' Approaching the communication with a sense of inquiry helps the client feel more comfortable, especially if the intuition challenges an aspect or role the client is identified with, a long-held belief, or where there may be fear or other strong emotions.

Checking In

Do not assume that what you're sensing is correct. If you do make this assumption, then you will no longer be supporting the client's agenda. If you notice this, then be mindfully aware of what is happening for you internally. Are you trying to prove your ability, trying to be right, trying to move this client ahead before they're ready?

Being Detached

Make sure that after you share what you're sensing you let go of it and follow what resonates for the client. Let go of the need to be right. It might happen that the client will later realise that what you have said made sense, however, if they don't resonate with it, then let it go. If you continue to attach to what you're sensing, you will likely trigger the client's limbic system, or at the very least, miss subtle nuances in what the client is trying to communicate.

Sometimes when you sense something, there is the impulse to immediately act on it by sharing it. This might be driven by your own need rather than checking in to make sure the timing is right for the client. You may sense that the client is not ready to hear it yet. Instead, you could write it down and share when it is more appropriate.

When you express your intuition, clients may disagree. Even so, they will learn as much as if your intuition were somehow "correct." What was correct was the intuition to say something.

What was correct was whatever the client learned. What's more, clients count on your intuition. When you hold back, you withhold a crucial source of information and sensing. The key lesson: do not be attached to your intuition, no matter how certain you feel. Being attached to being right is something you do for your sake. Coaching is for the sake of the client.

- Henry Kimsey-House and Karen Kimsey-House[15]

PRACTICE: Mindful Moment

Take a moment to practice mindfulness. Focus on your breath, your body, and your senses. Notice how you feel in this moment, the surrounding sounds, and the colours and textures of the surrounding objects. Bring acceptance to all that is within and around you.

Supporting Clients to Tune Into and Trust Intuition

As a coach, you can add an enormous amount of value to the coaching process by supporting the client to develop their intuitive ability. It is much more important for the client to learn how to tune in and trust their

---

15 Henry Kimsey-House and Karen Kimsey-House. *Co-Active Coaching* (2011).

intuition, rather than relying on you to share what you sense intuitively. Intuition is a valuable skill the client can continue using after the coaching and throughout their lives.

Here are a few ways to support clients to tune in and trust their intuition:

Mindfulness Practices

Support the client by bringing their attention to the present moment and introducing mindfulness practice. Start the session with a mindfulness practice so they can quiet their mind and more easily sense intuition.

Present Moment Awareness

Ask the client to notice what is happening in the present moment during the coaching session. Support them to sense the subtle signals of intuition. Ask a question about what they sense, hear, see, feel, etc. You could also simply ask, 'What is present for you as you talk about this topic?' or 'What is happening for you right now?'

Introducing the Idea of Intuition

It can be useful to discuss what intuition is with your clients and how they sense it, whether they trust intuition, and what might support them to tune in. You could send them articles or blog posts about intuition and its benefits. Also, include the science behind intuition and your experiences of tuning in and trusting intuition.

Invite the Client to Tune In

As they talk about an issue in a session, instead of asking them what they're thinking, or how they need to get to their goal, try asking them about their intuition. For example, you could ask, 'What does your intuition tell you?'

or 'What does your heart or gut tell you to do?' or more subtly, 'What are you sensing?'

Notice the Client's Energy

Notice the difference when a client's energy is in their 'head' and when they sense something intuitively. Usually, they will get to the point of thinking in circles. At this point, it can be useful to ask them to sense what their intuition is telling them, what is happening in their body, or how they're feeling. This way, you're bringing the focus and energy away from thinking, and focusing more on the subtle signals of the body and feelings.

Journal about Intuition

Suggest to the client they keep a journal to note any insights they may have about intuition. This journal could focus on the following aspects:

- how they sense intuition (e.g., bodily sensations, feelings, thoughts, images, etc.);

- what they notice about how intuition communicates (e.g., 'I'm sensing my intuition is telling me');

- noticing what happens when they do or don't trust intuition; and

- what supports them to tune in and trust their intuition (e.g., mindfulness, time for reflection, etc.)

Stream of Consciousness Writing

It can be helpful for clients to use a technique called 'stream of consciousness writing' to sense what their intuition is communicating. Usually, this starts with exploring a topic or asking a question, such as, 'What is the best decision in this situation?' then write without thinking about what they're writing. In other words, writing whatever comes to mind without filtering it. At first, it might be all conscious thoughts, however, eventually, you will probably notice more intuitive thoughts coming through the writing.

Supporting the Decision-making Process

Last week, I had a few clients present the same issue. They all identified they needed to make a decision about something in their lives. One client was trying to decide what workshops to run for her business; another was figuring out where to live; and another wasn't sure where to go next with her new business. They had thoroughly thought about the pros and cons of each option, but kept going around in circles with the different options and still couldn't make a decision. When I supported them to tune into their intuition, they could all easily see the direction they needed to go in.

As a coach, you can play a valuable role when supporting clients to access their intuition, particularly when making decisions. Here is a process I have discovered that works when supporting clients to make decisions.

1. Explore how it feels when they know a decision feels right. Ask them to think back to a time when they just knew the way forward. For example, in the past, one of the clients knew that when he was looking to rent a home, he knew straight away whether it was his next home or not, he could feel it. He felt relaxed, his thoughts were quiet, his belly felt expanded, and he felt a sense of joy and calm at the same time.

2. Explore how it feels when they know a decision doesn't feel right. Ask them to think back to a time when they knew a decision wasn't right or the way forward. One of the clients said he noticed that when a business decision doesn't feel right, he feels a contraction in his body, his thoughts are disconnected, he feels irritated and confused.

3. Explore decision-making based on intuition with small, everyday decisions. For example, when planning a day out, notice what feels good and what feels contracted. If it feels

contracted, it is unlikely to be the best way forward. Then start to explore it with bigger decisions.

Of course, it can take a bit of trial and error to be clear on what your intuition is telling you. It has taken a lot of playing with this in different areas of my life to become attuned to what feels right and what doesn't feel right. It's like fine tuning an instrument; it takes practice to know what it sounds like when it's tuned and when it doesn't sound right.

Guided Imagery Tools

You could also use guided imagery tools to support the client to tune into intuition. Try using the following guided practice with clients.

Guided Exercise: Intuitive Decision Path Exercise

Write down your specific decision and list the alternatives. Mark each alternative as 1, 2, 3, 4, and so on.

Sit down, close your eyes, and make yourself comfortable. Take a few deep breaths. Let go of the thoughts and distractions of the day.

Imagine yourself walking down an imaginary path. Take a few moments to notice the scenery. What season is it? How is the weather? What time of day is it? Are you enjoying this walk?

A short way ahead of you, the path breaks into a number of different paths. When you come to the place in the path where the road splits, stop.

Each path represents one of your alternatives. Number the paths in any direction comfortable to you and let those numbers correspond to the number of your alternatives.

Take your time, take a deep breath, and let it out slowly. Now, choose one of the paths as if you have decided to go with that alternative and slowly travel down that path. Notice how you feel. Call up your intuition and answer these questions:

What do you see on the path?

What are the feelings associated with the choice of path?

What are your physical sensations?

What is happening in your gut or heart? Is there a tightening or a gripping, or a softness, spaciousness, or warmth?

What sounds do you notice?

Notice your thoughts about the path-are they generally positive or negative?

Notice where the path takes you?

Take as long as you want to explore this path.

When you have finished, go back to the place where the paths meet. Choose another path and explore it as you did the first one. Continue exploring until you have experienced this path.

When you have finished, go back to the place where the paths meet and explore the next alternative path until you have completed each alternative.

Once you have finished, walk back up the road once again, noticing the scenery in as much detail as possible. Take another deep breath and let it out slowly. When you are ready, you can open your eyes and record the events of this exercise.

Debriefing with the client: The coach can interact with the client during the exercise or wait until the end to ask the client to describe what they sensed.

Some questions you can ask include:

What did you feel, see, hear, sense as you walked down each path?

Where did each path take you?

What did you notice about the difference between the paths?

Is there another path that hasn't been considered?

How does this knowledge inform you about your decision?

What actions would you like to take based on this new information?

Guided Exercise: Intuitive Coaching Dialogue

Firstly, create a list of questions you would like to ask your intuition. This may be a decision you need to make, an issue that is unresolved, or another topic you want to explore in more detail.

Now, imagine yourself as the intuitive self (i.e., that it is all knowing, doesn't need to think about the answers at all, and the answers come automatically, often from the body, heart or gut). As you feel your way to being the intuitive self, change your body position to reflect how you would sit as your intuitive self.

You're now in the position of the all-knowing, intuitive voice within and have all the answers to whatever questions you would like to ask. I will now ask you the first question you had. Take your time to sense your response, then let me know what it is you're sensing.

Coach to ask the question and then allow space for the client to respond. You might ask some follow-up questions if needed. Then check when the client feels complete with that question and move onto the next question.

If you notice the client tending to go back into their head to get the answers, getting confused, lacking clarity, emotionally triggered, then remind them to move back into the position of the intuitive voice.

The intuitive voice knows the answer to all the questions and doesn't waver at all when answering. If you notice yourself wavering or thinking too much, then you may need to adjust your body and place yourself back into being the intuitive self.

When you have the answers you need, thank your intuitive self and note the answers to your questions.

The coach can use whatever was discovered as the basis for the rest of the coaching conversation, supporting the client to gain clarity as to what their next steps should be.

Guided Exercise: Listening to the heart

Firstly, ask the client to bring to mind a situation they want some resolution about (e.g., a decision they need to make, a relationship they need to understand, or any issue they may be currently dealing with).

Then ask them to close their eyes and feel into their heart area (this gets them out of their mind) and ask them to remember a good memory or visualise a scene where they feel happy and relaxed.

Once they can visualise or remember the scene, ask them to describe what they see in vivid detail. When you feel they are more relaxed and at ease, ask them what their heart wants to say about the situation they identified earlier.

Encourage them to speak from their heart, in other words, the place that doesn't need to think, but simply knows the solution, or at least the next step. Be careful to make sure they stay connected to their heart. You can hear when they go back into thinking with the mind because they will often become confused and agitated about the situation again. Gently ask them to stay with the heart and remind them of the memory or visualisation if necessary.

Make sure you allow anything that comes up for them in this space. At first, it might seem ridiculous or irrational (and most probably will, because this is intuition, after all), but go with whatever comes up and keep asking questions to deepen what is being presented.

CHAPTER 6

CREATING NEW AWARENESS

Mindfulness creates new awareness

Mindfulness isn't just about knowing that you're hearing something, seeing something, or even observing that you're having a particular feeling. It's about doing so in a certain way – with balance and equanimity, and without judgment. Mindfulness is the practice of paying attention in a way that creates space for insight.

- Sharon Salzberg, *Real Happiness.*

Mindfulness creates space for new awareness. When we are stuck in the default mode, we become identified with an old story we have been playing in our minds, and it is difficult to generate new awareness.

Through being mindfully aware, we quiet down the mind chatter, the noise in the brain, and allow a new awareness to arise naturally. It isn't even a matter of thinking or trying to get to a solution; the solution naturally arises as a result of our present moment awareness.

Clients often arrive at a session with a noisy mind. By supporting them to quiet the mind, we support the client to reflect. This reflection stage is where the client reflects on the situation, rather than trying to think or create more noise around it.

By allowing the mind to go quiet, the client is better able to pick up on subtle signals in the moment and ultimately generate the 'aha!' or insight. The reflection needs to come before the insight. Without reflection, there is very little new insight. Instead, the solutions will be based on the old wiring of the brain and old ways of doing things, which might work in the short-term, however, won't create long-term change. What is needed is some new awareness, particularly in areas where a client is stuck.

You may often notice when you're intensively focused on thinking about a problem that it rarely helps with finding a solution. Instead, you dig more and more into the problem and become stressed because no new solution arises. However, you might notice that going for a walk, focusing on another task, having a shower, 'sleeping on it', or just switching off in some way, the solution soon arises like a light bulb going on in the dark. The solution arises because you have managed to allow the mind to go quiet, creating space for new connections to be made. Mindfulness supports clients to quiet the mind and have these light bulb moments.

Surface vs. Deeper Levels of Awareness

Surface level awareness tends to focus on the 'what' and 'how' of the situation. The conversation is about solving the issue in practical ways so that the client can move forward. This focus can be very useful, especially if the client has already gained plenty of awareness and insight into the situation and can see a way forward. However, it can also be limited if it is the only focus in the conversation.

Clients often come to coaching because they have something they want to achieve. However, they're unsure as to how to go about moving forward. They may know the 'how' and have still found it difficult to move forward. For example, a client that is consistently late to meetings may know many different time-management techniques, but he still turns up late to meetings. Therefore, the conversation needs to move to a deeper level of awareness to find out what is happening and generate new insights to create forward motion.

Exploring Deeper Levels of Awareness

By delving into deeper levels of awareness, we access what might unconsciously be driving the client and the issue. We need to be gentle, exploring with the client, rather than forcing them to see something they aren't ready to see yet.

Without the client being aware of what is going on unconsciously, they will continue to be driven by it. Even if they manage to solve an issue in one area, they will transfer this to another area. For example, a client might manage to sort out an issue with his boss, however, notice the same issue playing out at home with his spouse.

This approach isn't about healing these unconscious issues, but bringing the issues into awareness so they can be acknowledged and transformed if the client chooses. Usually, just acknowledging the pattern, belief, idea, feeling, or thought that was previously unconscious can shift the client's perspective and create enough energy to move forward.

Quiet Reflection

One essential element for creating depth in a conversation is providing space for quiet reflection, by allowing more silence. Enable the client to take the time to reflect on their thoughts before coming in with your next question or comment.

You will notice when a client is in reflection mode when they start to look upward as if trying to access new connections in their brain; they go quiet; they slow down their pace of talking, and they're more relaxed. You can support the client to reflect by flowing with the client's exploration, rather than bringing in your thoughts or ideas about where the conversation needs to go or trying to push them to get to insight. Allow yourself to sit in the uncertainty of reflection and trust that the client will be able to generate new awareness from this space.

Focus on Insight

As a coach, when we learn the objective of a coaching session is to create new awareness and insight, we attach to this idea, as a symbol or reflection of our value as coaches. The thought might be, 'The more awareness I can bring to support this client to create, the better I am as a coach.' We might start to think that if the client doesn't have any significant insights, we have failed as coaches. We have become identified with our thoughts about our value and achieving an outcome for the client, having lost our presence and connection to the moment in the conversation.

Sometimes a client won't have a major insight, and this may have nothing to do with your skill. It might be that the client isn't ready for an insight in this area, they could be resistant to seeing the core issue, or perhaps they have already gained plenty of insight from previous sessions, and it is time for integration of awareness into action.

The important point is to focus on being present and aware if you're making yourself responsible for the client's insights. If you're focused on needing the client to have insights so that you feel as if you have provided value, then you've lost your connection with being present, and you will miss the opportunities to support the client to gain awareness.

PRACTICE: Mindful Moment

Take a moment to practice mindfulness. Focus on your breath, your body, and your senses. Notice how you're feeling in this moment, the surrounding sounds, and the colours and textures of the surrounding objects. Bring acceptance to all that is within and around you.

Coaching the 'Who' and the 'What'

Conversations that generate a deeper level awareness tend to be focused more on the 'who' rather than the 'what'. The 'what' focuses on what the client *is learning about the situation*, as opposed to the 'who' which focuses on *what the client is learning about self.*

A coaching conversation focused on 'who' is about exploring with the client who they're being, their feelings, present moment experience, perceptions, beliefs, biases, and big-picture view. This type of conversation is internally focused, rather than an externally focused, which requires the client to be mindful of their internal experience.

For example, a 'what' conversation with a client that has work/life balance issues might logically focus on what she needs to do to bring her life back into balance. There are many solutions she might focus on, such as leaving work on time, switching off technology when she leaves the office, and scheduling in time for family and hobbies. Some of these solutions might work for a while, however, if we leave the factors underlying the work/life balance issue unacknowledged, sooner or later the issue is likely to come up again.

Instead, by focusing on the 'who' we can support the client to explore who she is being when she doesn't make time for her family and herself. Bringing mindfulness to her thoughts, feelings, body sensations, limiting beliefs, values and perceptions. This new awareness can support the client to shift into a new way of being.

Our inner state is not an accident. We can become familiar with it, eventually developing mastery in working with it. This mastery of our inner world is a requirement for our effectiveness and is key to accelerating our development as humans and as leaders. As coaches, the mastery is central to our ability to cultivate real and lasting change for our team members and our clients.

–Doug Silsbee, *Presence-Based Coaching.*

Awareness of the Core Issue

The client will often start the conversation with what they think is the issue. However, this isn't often the core issue. They might start with the surface level issue, and as the conversation deepens, they will start to understand the core issue or what is really behind this surface level issue.

Often asking a direct question is the easiest way to identify the core issue. Sometimes, they may not be ready to see it, so you can continue to explore and then ask again at a later stage of the conversation.

The other way to obtain the core issue is to clarify what you're hearing might be the core issue. Ask permission to share what you're sensing. Even if it isn't the core issue, the conversation often goes deeper because the client will be able to clarify what is and isn't the core issue, based on your sharing.

Often as coaches, we are taught to avoid the problem or the core issue, having been encouraged to stay on the surface level, where it is safe and logical. There might even be a feeling that delving too deeply into the problem or core issue might make the situation worse for the client, or that this is more for the areas of counselling and psychotherapy. However, it is possible to acknowledge the core issue, without delving into the emotional past, in a way that creates forward momentum for the client.

For example, a client who is late for meetings discovers this is a need for attention. He also acknowledges he had this behaviour when he was a child, looking for attention from his parents who were too busy with their careers to give him much time. This information about the past came spontaneously in the session; I didn't ask for this information. Rather, the client had a memory that connected him to the past.

In coaching, it is important to acknowledge the core issue of needing attention. However, it isn't necessary to delve into the client's childhood and the need for attention from his parents. Instead, it is possible to stay with what is present when he is late, what he senses, feels, hears, and notices. Use the mindfulness techniques to support the client to be aware of his experience when he is running late. He can then choose to change this behaviour once he has acknowledged what is driving it.

Awareness of Emotions

Mindfulness is about acknowledging the present moment in an open, accepting, and non-judgmental way. It includes acknowledging and accepting how we are feeling in the moment. Instead of pushing emotions away and judging them. When we can be present to emotions, we discover that they move and dissolve. A useful way to look at emotions is as 'energy in motion'. The emotions are just energy passing through, rather than something that is here to stay.

So, by supporting the client to develop mindfulness, they will become more aware of their emotions in the present moment and bring more loving acceptance to whatever is arising. You can also support them by asking them what is present and making space for them to feel and sense what is happening in the session.

Often as human beings, we are in the limbic mode, in other words, we are in the fight, flight, or freeze response. Due to the nature of the world we live in, our nervous system is often aroused, especially now that we have more and more contact with strangers, try to manage multiple tasks at one time, meet others' expectations, and the many other demands we place on ourselves. It isn't surprising that our clients often turn up for a session with an aroused limbic system. They may be in a whirlpool of emotions and their willingness to focus on drama is a sign they have 'gone limbic'.

By bringing mindful awareness to the session, you will support the client to calm their limbic system. They can then use the prefrontal region of the brain to generate new awareness, make connections, remember and learn. Being aware of this limbic arousal in a client and bringing attention to it can support the client to connect with themselves and generate deeper awareness.

Another way to support the client, apart from using mindfulness practices, is for you to provide them with a calm, clear, peaceful presence. There is research indicating that we have mirror neurons in the brain[16]. As humans, we tend to mirror the behaviour or energy around us or nearest to us. So, if someone is angry in the office, then everyone around this person will likely start to feel angry or annoyed, particularly with this person.

When we are present and able to hold the space for ourselves without mirroring other, strong emotions around us, then our clients, or those around us, will start to vibrate with that peaceful presence. You can feel when someone with this type of presence walks into a room, as everyone else seems to take a deep breath, relaxing and calming their nervous systems.

Labelling the Emotion

Another way of supporting the client when strong emotions are aroused is through labelling. When a strong emotion is aroused, the limbic system has been triggered and thus the prefrontal region which we use for making decisions, remembering, inhibiting thoughts, and learning diminishes in its ability to function. The client is focused on survival because they unconsciously feel threatened. To support the client to dampen this limbic system response, we can ask them to label the emotion. For example, if you could use a word to describe how you're feeling now, what would it be?

Letting go of the story

One important distinction is that we are not asking the client to express more of the story about the situation that triggered the emotion. Though this sometimes might be useful, it often leads the client to embed the story and get stuck in an emotional pattern. It is more useful to support them to be present, rather than lost in thought about the situation.

---

16 *Keysers, Christian; Gazzola, Valeria (2010).* "Social Neuroscience: Mirror Neurons recorded in Humans" *(PDF). Current Biology. 20 (8): R353–354.*

PRACTICE: Mindful Moment

Take a moment to practice mindfulness. Focus on your breath, your body, and your senses. Notice how you feel in this moment, the surrounding sounds, and the colours and textures of the surrounding objects. Bring acceptance to all that is within and around you.

Awareness of Thoughts

Internal Dialogue

The client's internal dialogue is often what gets in the way of the client moving forward. Clients often aren't aware of their internal dialogue and how it runs their lives. Developing more understanding and awareness can be useful in loosening the identification.

It can be particularly useful to be aware of the inner judge and inner child dialogue. This internal dialogue affects how we perceive life and situations. Mindful awareness, or standing back as a witness to the relationship between these two aspects, will support the client to shift their identification with one or both of these positions.

For example, consider a client who wants to follow her passion for interior design and start her own business, she has been working in corporate banking for the last ten years. The dialogue of the inner judge would typically be, 'Don't leave this job, it's safe and provides regular income. If you go out on your own you won't have enough money. Who is going to want what you have to offer? You're silly for even thinking about leaving.' You might notice this dialogue sounds like a parent protecting a child from doing something that might be dangerous. The inner judge is trying to keep us safe, in our comfort zones, and away from danger.

On the other hand, the inner child might typically respond to the inner judge or parent with a demanding voice, saying, 'I'm so sick of doing this boring job. I want to do my own thing and have my own time. It isn't fair that others have the money and resources to do what they want. I want to be able to do what I want!' The child is often impatient and wanting something now, rather than having to wait for it, reacting to the restriction imposed by the inner judge or parent.

We often identify with one or both of these positions. Usually, both go on internally, whether we are aware of it or not. It is useful in a session to support the client to see this internal dialogue playing out, noticing the different voices, and using the mindful witness to step back and see the relationship playing out between the two aspects.

Voice Dialogue is a technique that can be used to generate awareness about these inner parts of ourselves. You can support the client to sit in different positions and speak from both the inner judge and the child, one at a time, role-playing the conversation, and swapping positions to voice each part of the dialogue. Then, at some point, it is useful to ask the client to step into a neutral position, look at both parts, and witness the conversation from the point of view of the observer. By standing back to observe the conversation, the client will often gain insight into the relationship and what is going on between the two aspects. Once they are aware of the internal dialogue, they will be able to shift their perception through the witness.

For example, in the above scenario, the client can sit back and witness this dialogue between her inner judge and child about starting a new job and see the inner judge is trying to protect her from making a mistake. This may bring more compassion for this aspect of herself. She may also see that the child wants the freedom to follow her energy and passion. However, it is also true that if she just leaves her job without building up enough money and other resources, she will simply be in survival mode, unable to experience the joy of following her passion. So the understanding arises that she needs to take a more balanced approach, starting to build the business, saving money, and then set a date in six months to leave her job, rather than doing it now.

The main purpose of this is to bring mindful awareness to the inner dialogue going around and around in the client's psyche. Through this awareness, the shift can start to take place, and the client will be able to move forward with this new awareness.

Limiting Thoughts

Through the awareness of the internal dialogue, the client will start to create awareness around those thoughts or beliefs that are limiting or disempowering. Often these beliefs are so common in our culture that we may not even notice them in the conversation. For example, the client might say, 'I know work is meant to be hard, and I need to put in a lot of hours.' This belief might limit the client in the way they approach their life. If we highlight and maybe even ask, 'Is that true?' The client can examine whether this belief is true and if it serves them.

Clients often identify with thoughts or a story about what the situation was, who did what, how they felt, and whether they felt good or bad about themselves. The story or drama often prevents them from fully experiencing the moment and what they're truly feeling. For example, a client might tell you a story about how a colleague didn't turn up for a meeting, how this person was rude and how he felt hurt. The story prevents him from actually feeling the pain and moving on. The story keeps him in the drama, rather than letting the emotion move through.

As your clients start to develop mindfulness, you can start to develop a dialogue about their stories, and they will start to notice when they go into the story about a situation, rather than being fully present to their experience. You can then ask them, 'Is this the story?' Through the awareness that they have identified with a story, they can then be supported to drop into being present with all the feelings, bodily sensations, and thoughts associated with this story. The story drops away, and a new awareness arises about the situation.

Mindfulness supports you to loosen your identification with thoughts. As you notice your thoughts more and more, you will notice that most of our suffering is created because we believe a thought to be true, when in fact, it is simply a thought and nothing more. Though it may feel real, it is ultimately only our perception, and this can be changed or even dropped completely. Through practicing mindful awareness, I have noticed that, over time, I have a greater capacity to see a thought, like, 'I'm not good enough,' as merely a thought, rather than the truth.

Reframing the Thought

Reframing disempowering thoughts can be useful when working with limiting thoughts and emotions. Through mindful awareness, the client may start to notice that emotion has been generated through a negative thought, and reframing the thought can often bring about a shift in emotions. For example, say a client, after a feedback session about her coaching skills, feels upset and frustrated. She notices these emotions are connected to the thought that she isn't skilled enough as a coach. By reframing this thought to something that is still real for her, like, 'It's true I have more to learn, however, I'm a quick learner, so I can implement these changes easily,' she is then able to calm down and start to think more clearly.

We can also support the client to reframe the belief in a way that would be more empowering. For example, the above could be reframed to, 'Work can be easy, and I can manage it within work hours.' However, this isn't about finding a positive thought they don't believe. It is about finding a more empowering way of thinking about the situation that they do believe.

The best way to know whether a reframe has supported the client to shift their perception is to bring mindfulness to the body sensations. Ask the client to notice how their body feels when they think one way and then to notice how they feel after the reframe. If the client feels, for example, a shift from feeling contraction to expansion in the chest, then this means the reframe is a useful one. If there has been no shift, then this technique hasn't worked, and a new technique or reframe may be needed.

PRACTICE: Mindful Moment

Take a moment to practice mindfulness. Focus on your breath, your body, and your senses. Notice how you feel in this moment, the surrounding sounds, and the colours and textures of the surrounding objects. Bring acceptance to all that is within and around you.

Awareness of the Body

To use the "body" as the body sensed from inside. Of course, it is the same body that can be observed from outside. And it is more than sensations and observations. Your body feels the complexity of each situation, and enacts much of what you do all day without your needing to think about each move. What you think is of course important, but you think only a few things at one time. It is your body that totals up the whole situation and comes up with appropriate actions most of the time. Human bodies live immediately and directly in a situation.

–Eugene T. Gendlin[17]

The body is a greater source of information than the mind alone. The mind is limited in its capacity and can only think one thought at a time. The body constantly feels and senses the world around us. Thus the mind often simply reacts to what the body senses.

---

17 Eugene T. Gendlin. Focus-oriented Psychotherapy (1996).

The body is often neglected as a source of information during a coaching conversation. By supporting clients to focus on the body, we support them to uncover more information about the situation they are focusing on. They are then able to uncover new insights.

During a coaching conversation, it can be useful to ask the client to connect with the 'felt sense' associated with everything they experience. The felt sense is the bodily interpretation of a situation, problem or issue. It is an inner awareness of the body that supports the client to experience what is below their awareness, however, not below the awareness of the body.

By supporting the client to focus on the 'felt sense' and describing what they're sensing in the body, they will get to the point where there is a 'felt shift'. This shift is when the client can name the felt sense, and by naming it, they experience it. The client usually feels some relief, joy, relaxation, contentment, or letting go.

If you think about when you've had an insight, you may have noticed you felt something shift. You might have felt stuck, then quietly reflective, and then excited, relieved, lighter, or joyful as you made the new connection. This is a felt sense shift. The mind shifted and so has the body.

Mindfulness is focused on bringing awareness to all aspects of our current moment experience. This includes bringing acceptance, openness, and non-judgment to experience as it is in the body. For example, a client might notice she feels tension in her body as she talks about a situation at work with her boss. Instead of focusing on the situation at work, encourage the client to feel what is happening in the body more, by asking her to describe this contraction more.

Coach: Can you describe the tension a bit more?

Client: It just feels like my body is tensing up talking about this situation. (The client is in limbic arousal.)

Coach: Where do you feel the tension? (By asking specifically where the tension is, the coach is asking the client to be in the moment, rather than in default mode about this issue. This then supports the client to dampen the limbic response. All the questions from now on continue the process of dampening the limbic response and allowing the client space to open up to new awareness.)

Client: In my heart. It feels like my heart is contracted and withdrawn.

Coach: Can you describe the feeling of contraction and being withdrawn?

Client: I feel like I'm curling in on myself, protecting myself from something.

Coach: What do you feel like you're protecting yourself from?

Client: Being hurt again. Yes, I'm protecting myself from the pain. Now I can start to feel the pain in my heart. It's already there. I was just protecting myself from feeling it.

Coach: Does it feel okay to give that feeling a bit more space? (Bringing some acceptance, openness, and not judging it for being there. Supporting the client to bring mindfulness to the uncomfortable feeling of pain, which is ultimately the core of what she has been avoiding feeling.)

Client: Yes, that feels okay. (There is some silence as the client feels this pain.)

Coach: What are you noticing as you feel this hurt or pain?

Client: I notice that as I give it more space, it starts to get lighter, easier to manage. (The client has experienced a shift.)

Coach: So it gets lighter and easier to manage. Anything else?

Client: Yes, I notice that I don't need to protect myself from this pain, that it isn't this big, scary feeling. It is something I can be with.

Coach: So it feels more like you're able to face it.

Client: Yes, and I just had an insight that my boss is also protecting herself. She is acting in this way to avoid feeling the same thing. I don't know how I know this, but it feels right. This gives me more compassion for her, and I think I'm now clear how I can approach this situation differently, in a way that will work for both of us.

The client, through bringing awareness to the body, had a shift in how she was feeling. Instead of avoiding the pain, she was able to make space for it and then when the resistance to the hurt or pain lightened, there was enough space for new awareness to arise. The new insight came easily, without needing to think about solutions.

For those with little awareness of the body, it can be more difficult to sustain awareness of the body and feel a shift. However, over time, with the development of mindfulness, this can happen. Sometimes it is enough to start to bring the clients attention to the body and learn the language of the body.

By starting to support your clients to develop this dialogue with the body, you're supporting them to move away from the identification with thoughts and more into the wisdom of the body. However, this does take time, so ensure you maintain your mindfulness as you support your clients to go through this process.

Embodiment of Awareness

Somatic Coaching considers that people do not necessarily change because they have gained knowledge; they change because they engage in new practices that change who they are. This means embodying what you learn in a physical way, and not just acquiring cognitively new information.

–Richard Strozzi-Heckler.[18]

To embody means to give bodily form. Often clients have a new awareness and understanding about a situation, however, somehow they still find it difficult to implement this new awareness. Often this is because there is only an intellectual understanding, rather than fully embodying the new awareness.

For example, a client who knows that he needs to lose weight for health reasons understands all the benefits and yet still doesn't take action. His

18 Richard Strozzi-Heckler. The Art of Somatic Coaching (2014)

awareness is only on an intellectual level; it has yet to become a full experience for him. If we start to bring mindfulness to his connection with the body, then we can start to understand the patterns of the body, how he feels about his body, and create new awareness from connecting with the body.

You can sense when someone has fully embodied a new understanding or awareness. For example, the manager who has an insight that he needs to be present to listen carefully to his staff and their needs. At first, he may revert to old behaviours of being distracted while listening, and it might take some conscious effort to rewire himself for this new way of being. Through awareness of his body, emotions, and thoughts, he can start to gain awareness about when he is and isn't present.

After he's noticed this for a while, he will start to embody this new presence, as it will be fully embedded as a way of being. He will simply relax and present without needing to think consciously about being present or listening carefully. He will be aware that when he is present, his body is relaxed, he feels curious, light, and connected. Thus, he will have fully embodied this way of being.

To be able to embody knowledge or new awareness, we need to connect to the body. When a client has an insight or new awareness about something, it can be useful to check in to see if she can feel it in the body and to describe what is happening in the body. The connection to the body will support the client to implement the new awareness in her life.

PRACTICE: Mindful Moment

Take a moment to practice mindfulness. Focus on your breath, your body, and your senses. Notice how you feel in this moment, the surrounding sounds, and the colours and textures of the surrounding objects. Bring acceptance to all that is within and around you.

Awareness of Habits

Habits are simply our repetitive reactions to an external stimulus. We see, hear, smell, taste, hear something we do or don't like, we then react based on how we feel.

Bringing mindfulness to habits can support the client to gently shift any embedded habits. Sometimes, the client might not be aware she is habitually doing the same thing over and over. We can support the client to become mindful of her habitual behaviours, thoughts, or feelings.

Instead of trying to change the habit immediately, it can be useful to first bring awareness to the habit without changing it. For example, a client who has an issue with overspending and she wants to create a new habit of budgeting. Before trying to change the habit, it's useful to spend some time bringing mindful awareness to the habit as it is now. To notice what happens as she spends too much, how it feels to have a large credit card bill or to borrow more money. To notice how she is feeling when she decides to buy something she can't afford, as well as exploring her relationship with money.

By bringing mindful awareness to the habit, the client can discover what is driving the behaviour. This new awareness is more likely to shift the behaviour, quickly and easily. If the client is aware that they tend to overspend when she needs to feel some joy in her life and that she feels depressed a day later, then she is more likely to look for the joy elsewhere, for example, in the joy of saving money, being debt free, and so on. Without this awareness, budgeting may feel very restrictive, and she may resent having to take on the new behaviour. Thus it is unlikely to continue in the long term.

Mindfulness allows us to bring awareness to these habits, to allow the client to notice when the behaviour, thought, or feeling arises, as well as the impact both on themselves and others. This new awareness gives the client a choice about what they would like to create in the future.

Blind Spots

Blind spots are usually habitual ways of doing, speaking, thinking, or feeling, that prevent the client from moving forward. By listening deeply with presence, a coach can clarify these blind spots in a way that allows the client to see and possibly transform them through simply being aware.

Blind spots are often shadowed aspects or qualities the client either doesn't like acknowledging about themselves or completely disowns. For example, say the client has a habit of being manipulative in relationships. They are blind to the shadow aspect of being manipulative, often saying, 'This isn't part of who I am,' and that they are being helpful or supportive, rather than manipulative. This shadow, or disowned aspect, often has a way of asserting itself in the client's life, especially when mirrored in another person.

It can be useful to support the client to bring mindfulness to these different aspects. However, we need to be able to do this with acceptance, openness, and non-judgment, otherwise, the client will likely feel judged.

Exploring blind spots can be tricky territory for a coach because there is a reason blind spots and shadow aspects are kept hidden - they are often too much for the client to see, as the ego has created this blindness to protect the client from experiencing pain. For example, if a client constantly supports her children and feels resentful toward them for not reciprocating or being grateful, she may not be able to see this behaviour as disempowering. She may be blind to this need to be loved by her children, and that she supports them to get love from them. She isn't doing it out of unconditional love. Rather, she wants something in return and is being manipulative to get what she wants. The children end up feeling manipulated and resentful of her constant need for love and attention. She is blind to the manipulation and her need to love herself, so she projects the source of love onto her kids instead of looking for it within herself.

Ideally, it is best if the client can generate her awareness of these blind spots, rather than having the coach point them out to the client. Support her to explore it deeper, to see what new awareness is generated. We may see a blind spot. However, we may also come to the wrong conclusion about the blind spot, or deliver it in a way that implies judgment, which is ultimately what the client fears the most.

Of course, with enough trust and openness, there are times when a client has generated enough awareness and is open to hearing what you sense. This goes back to the chapter on intuition and sharing what you're sensing without assuming you are right, checking with the client to make sure it resonates, as well as letting it go if it doesn't.

Blind spots can also include essential qualities or strengths that the client doesn't acknowledge. By bringing more mindful awareness to these qualities, they can strengthen and build on these essential qualities. As coaches, we can reflect back these qualities - such as strength, willpower, compassion, courage, love, vulnerability, peacefulness, stillness, calm, and enthusiasm - when we see them in the client. By acknowledging that you, as the coach sense qualities, or if you hear the client say they sense a quality within themselves, you can ask the client to bring more mindful awareness to these qualities. By giving them more attention in the moment, the energy tends to expand and grow.

I have noticed this in my mindfulness practice. When I close my eyes and go in, there is a stillness and a sense of peace and strength, internally. I might also notice thoughts trying to distract me from sensing these essential qualities. However, over time I have learned to give more attention to this internal space and thus the stillness, peace, and strength within has expanded. I have given it more space than I would normally have given my identification with thoughts, and thus I'm more aware of these qualities within myself.

As a coach, you have the same capacity to bring your client's attention to these essential qualities, so they can have more space within, and be reflected in their external life. For example, the more I feel the stillness and peace within, the greater capacity I have to deal with any external challenges that come along. I no longer identify as much with the thoughts about these challenges. I have a greater awareness that I can just go in and be connected with this peace that is always there, no matter what is going on in my external world.

Awareness of Patterns or Themes

Highlighting patterns in words, thoughts, feelings, or connections across the conversation supports the client to generate new levels of awareness. Often the client isn't aware of these themes, so we can add value by listening deeply with mindfulness, to feel and sense these patterns as they arise, such as a client that repetitively uses a word in the conversation, or goes blank when they try to think about a situation.

To sense these patterns, we need have a quiet mind. If we're thinking about the next question, where to go in the conversation, or any other internal dialogue, then we will miss these themes or patterns.

PRACTICE: Mindful Moment

Take a moment to practice mindfulness. Focus on your breath, your body, and your senses. Notice how you feel in this moment, the surrounding sounds, and the colours and textures of the surrounding objects. Bring acceptance to all that is within and around you.

Creating Awareness through Analogies

Analogies can be very useful for supporting clients to be present with their experiences and shift their perspective. An analogy[19] 'is a

---

19 Definition sourced from https://en.oxforddictionaries.com

comparison between one thing and another, for the purpose of explanation or clarification.'

As coaches, most of the time we compare how the client is feeling in a situation to an image or visual representation of what is happening. For example, the client is feeling like a work situation is like being on a battlefield, or that leaving a job feels like jumping off a cliff into the unknown.

Using visual language allows the client to shift perspective and think about things that might normally be difficult to think about. Exploring an analogy with the client allows them to gain some clarity of distance from the issue. It becomes less personal, and so they're able to create new awareness.

For example, if a client feels burdened by everything he needs to achieve every day, never feeling like he can make progress, and exhausted from working so hard, the analogy you might sense is the client carrying the world on his back up a big mountain and having no choice but to carry it. You can see if this analogy resonates with the client and then explore it to gain a new perspective.

Bringing mindfulness to the analogy also adds a level of experiencing and possibly creating a shift. For example, supporting the client to focus on creating awareness as to how it feels to carry the world on his back. What does he sense emotionally and physically? It can be useful to ask him to assume the position of holding the world on his back. What does he notice while in this position? Then if he feels to let go of the world on his back, asking him to notice what that feels like in comparison.

Other questions you might ask include: What he senses this man carrying the world on his back needs to do? After looking at him, what would he advise? He might need to drop it, share it, or take an easier route up the mountain.

At some point, you will then need to ask the client to link it back to the current situation. For example, if you decide to take an easier route up the mountain. How does this look in his everyday life? Perhaps he needs to focus on doing less each day and pacing himself throughout each day by taking short breaks.

The best analogies are the clients' analogies. We can support our clients by building on the analogies they provide. For example, if a client says she feels like she is on a sinking ship, you could ask, 'Can you describe this image of being on a sinking ship more,' or 'So, if you're on a sinking ship, what would be the best way to save yourself?' or 'If you're on a sinking ship, look around - what do you notice?' or 'Describe this feeling of being on a sinking ship more - what do you notice about the ship? Are there people around? What do you sense physically and emotionally?' Use the words the client has mentioned to build on the image.

The client's dialogue in conversation with you is full of potential analogies. We often use visual language to describe our situation, so as coaches, we just need to be present enough to pick up on them. Often the language a client uses is indicative of what is happening in the moment and provides the key to moving forward.

Another way to work with analogies is to ask the client to come up with an example for the current situation they're describing. You will first need to make sure they have a connection with their visual sense. You could then ask them to close their eyes and to describe their feelings using an image.

Here's an example of coaching with an analogy:

Client: I feel like I'm ready to take a leap into the unknown. However, I feel like I can't quite let go. (Client has her own business and has noticed the growth has been limited, and she needs to take it to a new level, however, doesn't know what to do.)

Coach: What do you want to happen?

Client: I want to take the leap, but I'm scared (connecting to the emotional experience).

Coach: Where do you feel this sensation?

Client: I feel it in my gut. It's like a contraction in my belly like I'm holding the energy in (connecting with the experience in the body).

Coach: Describe more what you see and feel.

Client: I see myself on the edge of a cliff, overlooking the sea. I'm ready to jump into the water and immerse myself in the ocean. However, I can't let go. I'm hanging on with my feet, but my body is leaning over.

Coach: What do you imagine will happen when you let go?

Client: I might drown and not be able to handle this enormous ocean.

Coach: Is there anything you need for support so you don't drown and can handle being in the ocean?

Client: Yes, I need fish gills so I can swim easily.

Coach: How would you go about getting fish gills?

Client: I need to eat Gillyweed! (A reference to a Harry Potter book where he eats a seaweed substance called Gillyweed and temporarily grows fish gills. There is laughter from the client at this point, which is usually a good indication an insight is coming, as it relaxes the client and allows her to release any resistance that has been preventing the insight.)

Coach: So how would you go about getting those?

Client: In the book, his very loyal friend gives him the Gillyweed. I need support! I need to ask others for support! I've been trying to do this all on my own and haven't been asking for support. I need to reach out, which means saying I don't know how to swim yet, but I'm willing to learn, and I need to reach out to others to support me. Wow! I didn't see that coming. (Client has generated a new awareness.)

Coach: So what is your insight from this analogy of taking the leap into the unknown? (Making a connection with the issue.)

Client: I need to stop thinking I have to do this all on my own. A friend who has a great network asked me only yesterday if I needed help marketing my business and I declined because I didn't want to impose on her. Now I real-ise I could have said, 'Yes!'

As you explore the analogy with the client, she will develop more under-standing of the situation, and there will eventually be a new insight or awareness. The client will also likely feel this in her body, so support her to identify the full experience as it shifts. Connecting the analogy or image to a felt sense will support the client to embody what she is sensing in the moment.

PRACTICE: Mindful Moment

Take a moment to practice mindfulness. Focus on your breath, your body, and your senses. Notice how you feel in this moment, the surrounding sounds, and the colours and textures of surrounding objects. Bring acceptance to all that is within and around you.

• CHAPTER 7 •

ASKING QUESTIONS
WITH MINDFULNESS

Powerful Questions to Generate Awareness

As coaches, we often think we need to have a list of powerful questions to support clients to achieve their desired outcomes. While it can be useful to have a toolkit of powerful questions, it is limiting if you use the questions in a way that is disconnected from what is happening coaching conversation.

If you're thinking about the next best question to ask, then you will miss the subtle cues that will support the client to generate a deeper level of awareness. You won't notice the energy, emotions, and tone of voice. Instead, you will deliver what you think is a powerful question. Even though these questions might be useful, they will be disconnected from the flow of the conversation, and thus not the most powerful for creating awareness and supporting the client.

Presence and Deep Listening

The most powerful questions come from a place of presence and deep listening. Instead of focusing on the next best question to ask, focus on being present when the client is speaking. Take a moment to respond after the client has spoken so that you can feel and sense your response before delivering it. It's almost like you're listening for the client to give you the question, rather than you being the one that has to come up with the question. This way, you are working together in partnership to create the questions. The questions that arise will tend to be open-ended, explorative, and intuitive. They explore what the client says and doesn't say, so a deeper level of awareness is generated.

Being Curious, Open, and Light

When we ask questions from presence, there tends to be a lightness and openness in the questions that arises from curiosity and exploration. Here is a quote from A.H. Almaas about inquiry. This form of inquiry is about exploring our present moment experience so that we can gain a deeper connection with our essential being or true self.

If we understand that inquiry springs out of the lightness and openness of joyful curiosity, we begin to see that the heaviness and seriousness are not characteristic of inquiry itself. They are only characteristic of some of the content that arises in inquiry and from the beliefs we have about it. So the content can be very happy or very painful, but the attitude of the inquiry itself doesn't have to be influenced by the content. The inquiry itself is an expression of openness, lightness, curiosity and love.

–A.H. Almaas *Spacecruiser Inquiry.*

Following the Thread of the Client

By staying present with the client and asking questions based on the listening, you're following the client's process or thread. It's like unravelling a woollen ball and following the thread to see where it will lead. To follow the threat we need to relax into the uncertainty of not knowing where the client is going or where the conversation is headed. Trusting that what gets unravelled or unpacked is perfect for the client's process.

Formula and Leading Questions

Formula questions (questions you have already determined before the conversation will be useful) or leading questions (questions that lead the client in a particular direction or to a solution you think works best) are examples of questions that often interfere with the client's thread or process. They tend to be based on your thinking about what you think the client should do. This need to use formula or leading questions can be very subtle. It is useful to bring awareness to what is happening for you, in the moment, when you feel the need to resort to these questions, as well as noticing what happens when you ask these questions.

Detailed Questions

If you notice yourself asking detailed questions to obtain information, then it's likely you're doing this so you can solve the issue for the client. It's often surprising how little information a coach needs about a situation and how asking an open question based on presence and intuition is much more powerful in supporting the client to get to the outcome for the session.

Simple Succinct Questions

Often the simplest questions are the best, those questions delivered directly and in a few words. These type of questions allow the client to continue their exploration without being redirected or coming out of their present moment experience. When we ask a simple question, the client can continue to deepen what is arising instead of being interrupted from their process.

When a client is in reflection mode, there is usually an insight arising in the background, coming to conscious awareness. If we ask a question that is too long or redirects the conversation, the insight that was arising might be lost, and the client might lose their connection with what had been arising from their unconscious into awareness.

PRACTICE: Mindful Moment

Take a moment to practice mindfulness. Focus on your breath, your body, and your senses. Notice how you feel in this moment, the surrounding sounds, and the colours and textures of the surrounding objects. Bring acceptance to all that is within and around you.

WHO and WHAT Questions

Focusing on the WHO means focusing on what the client is learning about themselves, including their perceptions, behaviours, intuition, bodily sensations, feelings, and so on. It is more about the internal process of the client to shift the external situation. Here are some examples of simple questions, based on supporting the client to explore the present moment and generate deeper levels of awareness about the WHO.

Present Moment Experience

Can you describe what is present for you right now?

How do you feel when this issue arises?

How do you feel as you talk about this issue?

Where do you feel the issue in your body?

What does this issue feel like? Can you describe the sensations?

What is your experience in the moment around this issue?

What is present for you when you talk about this issue?

If you could give me an image of what you're sensing right now, what would it be?

Can you describe the issue using your senses?

What do you see, feel, hear, and sense as you explore this issue?

What arises in your experience when you notice this is an issue?

As you talk about and experience this issue, what are you noticing?

What do you sense is contributing to this issue?

What is the inner dialogue you have running about this issue?

What thoughts are going on in the back of your head as you talk about this issue?

What feels different now that you've said that aloud?

What do you notice about your body when you think about this issue?

What image or analogy would you use to describe what you're experiencing in this situation?

Who is the Client Being?

How are you contributing to this issue?

Who are you being in relation to this issue?

Who would you like to be in relation to this issue?

What is the impact, both internally and externally?

How do you benefit from continuing to have this issue?

What could you shift in yourself to shift this situation or issue?

What do you know about yourself that could be applied in this circumstance?

What do you need to shift internally to resolve this issue?

What deeper understanding about yourself would support you right now?

Core Issue

What is the core issue?

What is behind this issue?

Are you willing to look deeper into this issue?

What is the deeper issue, beyond the issue of...?

What is the core of this for you?

Intuition

What does your gut tell you about this issue?

If your gut could talk, what would it say?

What does your heart say is going on in this area?

What do you sense your intuition is telling you about this situation?

What is your inner voice telling you about this issue?

Reframing Questions

How could you shift your perspective in this area?

If you could look at this from a third person perspective, what do you think you would see about yourself?

If you could zoom out and look at this issue from afar, what do you think you would notice about yourself?

If a good friend came to you for advice on this same issue, what would you tell them?

Insights About Self

Is there a theme to what you have discovered? If so, what would that theme be?

How are you feeling now, compared to when you started this conversation?

What are you learning about yourself in this conversation?

How could you apply this new learning about yourself?

What new insights do you have from this conversation?

The WHAT in the conversation is about focusing on what the client is learning about the situation, including what they can do to move forward, options, goals, and outcomes. The emphasis is on the external practicalities of the situation and solution. This focus is particularly useful when the client has shifted their awareness and is ready to apply the new awareness to the current situation.

Examples of questions would be:

What is the situation or issue?

What would you like to achieve by the end of this session?

What do you think the solution is?

What can you do to change the situation?

What are your options?

What do you want to commit to doing in the next week?

What do you want to do regarding your goals?

How can you keep yourself accountable?

How you can you support yourself to make sure you get these actions done?

Have you tried an alternative approach? What were the results?

What have you done in the past? What were the results?

Based on this insight, what do you think would be the next step forward for you?

What is your plan for achieving these targets?

Now that you have had this new insight, what do you think you can do about it?

What planning do we need to implement to ensure your success in this area?

What are your options based on this insight?

Do you have a plan for moving forward in this area?

How clear is your plan for achieving this objective?

What are the milestones for achieving this goal?

What are the major steps for achieving your goal?

What are you prepared to do to make this goal happen?

What are some of the alternatives for moving forward in this goal area?

Do you want to take some action around this?

What is one step you could take towards that this week?

How can you apply that insight into other areas of your life now?

What will you complete by next week?

PRACTICE: Mindful Moment

Take a moment to practice mindfulness. Focus on your breath, your body, and your senses. Notice how you feel in this moment, the surrounding sounds, and the colours and textures of the surrounding objects. Bring acceptance to all that is within and around you.

• CHAPTER 8 •

SUPPORTING CLIENTS TO DEVELOP MINDFULNESS

Introducing Mindfulness to your Clients

Sometimes clients will readily embrace mindfulness, and others will have doubts about what the benefits of applying mindfulness will be. I often hear from clients or participants in programs that they're okay the way they are, so why do they need to learn mindfulness? Often these individuals aren't aware of the impact the constant stream of rumination has on their psychological and physical wellbeing. Also, change can be hard and mindfulness, although simple to explain, isn't easy to apply on a consistent basis.

What do they know?

Since mindfulness is becoming more and more popular and many more people know about it, most clients will have likely come across the term. So when you decide to introduce clients to mindfulness, it is important to find out what they know about mindfulness and whether they practice mindfulness. Then, based on what they do or don't know, you can inform them about mindfulness and the benefits.

Find a Common Language

It can be useful to find a common language the client can relate to, for example, instead of introducing the practice as mindfulness, you can use words the client relates to, for example, focusing or centring exercise.

Highlight the Benefits

As you understand more about the client's situation, you will more clearly understand the possible benefits of applying mindfulness that they would be interested in, so you can relate these benefits to their current situation.

Referencing scientific studies on benefits of mindfulness gives it more credibility, and thus clients might be more inclined to try it out. For example, if a client is having issues being reactive with her team members, you could point out studies showing that mindfulness supports individuals to respond to situations rather than react, which could be useful in her dealings with staff.

Also, sharing your experience of applying mindfulness can be effective in communicating the benefits, as well as sending them an article about mindfulness.

Part of the Coaching Process

Often I introduce the topic of mindfulness at the beginning of a coaching series when I talk to the client about the coaching process. I explain that this practice is part of the coaching and that we will be going through a mindfulness practice at the beginning of every session for a few minutes. I explain this will support her to focus during the coaching session and get the most out of the coaching series.

Right Timing

With some clients, you will automatically sense they are open to mindfulness and what it could bring to their lives. With other clients, however, you might be unsure as to whether you should introduce the idea of mindfulness. Often it can be useful to feel into the right timing, notice what the client talks about and at some point, the conversation may lend itself to a conversation about mindfulness. For example, if the client is talking about how he can't focus and finds himself continually distracted, then you could suggest that mindfulness might help to support him to focus.

Guiding your Client through a Mindfulness Practice

There are few steps to guiding a client through a mindfulness practice:

1. Set up: Explain that during the exercise they can either keep their eyes open or closed and to find a comfortable position in which to sit.

2. Timing: Let them know how long the mindfulness practice will be or ask them how long they would like to go for. I sometimes find that clients love this part of the session and want up to 10 minutes because it's the only time of the day they get to practice being present. Others are happy with one or two minutes. Adjust the mindfulness practice to suit the timing.

3. Describe the process: Outline what the mindfulness practice is and where they need to focus.

    For example, you could say the following *'I will guide you through by asking you to focus on your breath and then on the different parts of the body, starting with your feet and moving up to the top of your head. As we go through each part of the body, notice any bodily sensations you become aware of. You don't need to force this awareness, simply lightly focus your attention on each part of the body. When you notice yourself getting distracted and going into default mode, gently bring yourself back to the body, once again noticing the bodily sensations.'*

I will finish by asking you to focus on the breath and then letting you know you can open your eyes. However, there is no rush to open your eyes - take your time and come back when you feel ready'.

4. Check to see if they have any questions and whether they are ready to start.

5. Guide them through the practice, making sure you're present as you do. Going through this practice will support you in being present for the client during the coaching session, so make sure you use the time to be mindful.

   At first you might like using one of the transcripts at the end of this book, however, after having used a variety of mindfulness practices, you might use your intuition to guide you with the words. I often find my intuition will guide me to say something different with a client, depending on where I'm being guided. For example, sometimes at the end of the mindfulness practice, I ask the client to feel into the heart area and sense an intention for the session, asking them to be guided by their intuition and heart about the intention and focus of the session.

6. Debrief after the practice. Check in with the client to find out what they experienced during the practice. Ask them whether there was anything in particular that drew their attention, what they noticed about the mind wandering, and anything else they sensed might have been important. Often what arises in the mindfulness practice will be a good lead into the session because the client has become aware of something they need to focus on for the session.

For example, a client was ready to talk about how to market her business and instead, through the mindfulness practice, becomes aware she is exhausted. Through further discussion, after the mindfulness practice, she acknowledges she needs to make herself a priority - how will she attract new clients and deliver if she is depleted? By going inward, she has created new awareness that was previously unseen because she was so identified with her thoughts about what she had to do, rather than what she needed.

PRACTICE: Mindful Moment

Take a moment to practice mindfulness. Focus on your breath, your body, and your senses. Notice how you feel in this moment, the surrounding sounds, and the colours and textures of the surrounding objects. Bring acceptance to all that is within and around you.

Supporting Clients to Develop Mindfulness

Mindfulness Exercises in the Session

There are many ways to support a client to develop mindfulness. You could use a mindfulness practice, such as focusing on the breath, body scan, senses exercises, and so on. The transcript for each of these exercises is in the last part of this book. These exercises can be applied at the beginning of the session or during the session if you notice the client is getting stuck or confused.

Mindfulness Questions

The other way to support the client to develop mindfulness is to ask questions that support the client to focus on their present moment experience during the session. Ask questions that focus on their internal thoughts, feelings, bodily sensations, and senses, or ask them what is happening in the moment as they talk about an issue. For examples of these questions, refer to Chapter 7.

Reflecting the Present Moment

By reflecting back to the client what you sense in the moment - such as the energy, emotions, body language, and tone of voice - can be useful to support the client to be present to her experience. For example, you could say, 'I noticed you hesitated before you spoke - what was happening for you in that moment?'

Clients won't often notice they have made a particular gesture in the moment or they have used a certain word to describe their experiences, so bringing their attention to what they did or said in the moment brings the focus into the here and now. This presence quiets the mind, so they can be more reflective, and thus generate more awareness.

Excessive Focus on the Future or Past

It can be particularly useful to notice if the client consistently projects into the future or goes into the past. There is nothing wrong with this tendency, however, if it doesn't support them to gain clarity and insight, then it can be more effective to bring their focus into the present moment.

It can be useful to notice when the client is lost in rumination, repetitive thoughts, and going around in circles. A coaching conversation can either continue this process of rumination or support the client to drop into a space of reflection and presence.

Internal exploration

With permission and placement, it can be useful to support the client to close their eyes and sense their internal experiences. It is usually easier to sense what is going on with the eyes closed. You can close your eyes at the same time, so the client feels more comfortable. Ask the client what they notice about their bodies, their feelings, and whatever comes into their awareness as they go in.

If they have been focusing on a particular issue, you can ask them to feel into where they feel it in the body. For example, perhaps a client feels his chest is tight, or maybe he feels anxiety in his stomach. You might also ask him to continue sensing and feeling what arises as he continues to stay present to how he is feeling and what he is sensing.

Practice Outside of the Session

The other way to support clients to develop mindfulness is to provide recordings and transcripts of mindfulness practices so that they can practice outside of the session. It is useful to suggest to the client they do some research to find a practice they enjoy. There are many books, audio recordings, courses, and phone apps available to support clients. Two of the most popular Apps are Insight Timer and Headspace.

Space, Silence, and Slower Pace

Providing space, silence, and a slower pace allows the client to be more present and reflect on their experience so that they can gain further awareness. They can then become aware of and listen to the subtle signals in their inner world. Often it is the gaps in the conversation that are the most powerful part. Without these gaps, the client isn't able to listen to these subtle signals and create new connections.

You Being Mindful

The most powerful way to support clients to develop mindfulness is for you to be mindfully present in the session. When you're vibrating a feeling of calm presence, the client will naturally start to vibrate with the same energy. They will start to feel calm, relaxed, and present, without you having to do or say anything in particular.

Creating New Habits

It isn't enough to focus on changing a habit; we also have to be more mindful as we notice ourselves moving into a default habit. By bringing awareness to the habit, noticing what happens for us emotionally and physically, the thoughts we have, the impact we have on others, we are more likely to change the habit through this awareness.

In a TEDMED talk, Judson Brewer[20] mentioned a study where they taught mindfulness to smokers. When one smoker became mindful of her smoking, she said, 'mindful smoking smells like stinky cheese and tastes like chemicals. Yuck!' The study had proven successful in supporting participants to quit smoking as well as if they had gone through gold standard therapy.

So, a first step in supporting clients to change habits is to support them to bring a more mindful awareness to the habits. Instead of trying to force behaviour changes, ask them to be aware of their thoughts, emotions, bodily sensations, and anything else they notice before, during or after, they go into the default of the habit.

For example, a client who eats compulsively at night and has put on excessive weight due to this habit. Through mindful awareness, she notices that when she feels the impulse to eat at night, she feels lonely. There is a sensation of emptiness in the pit of her stomach and feelings of unworthiness arise. All of this would happen before she went to the fridge and she would

---

20 https://www.ted.com/talks/judson_brewer_a_simple_way_to_break_a_bad_habit

start to feel better while she was eating the food, as well as more hopeful, and less lonely and anxious. However, as soon as she finished, she would feel herself judging that she had, once again, been eating at night.

By seeing this sequence of events, she became aware that the root of it was this loneliness she felt at night and that she felt depleted, exhausted, and undernourished. From this, she started to become aware of her feelings of loneliness as emotions, which pass through if felt. She also started to nourish herself more at night by having a bath, taking care of herself, practicing mindfulness, reconnecting with friends and family, going out for dinner, or whatever else would help her to feel more nourished and connected to herself.

It can also be useful to bring mindful awareness to the client's experience as they change the habit. Exploring what arises in their experience as they try something new. For example, what thoughts, feelings and body sensations arise when the above client starts to spend time nourishing and connecting with herself.

PRACTICE: Mindful Moment

Take a moment to practice mindfulness. Focus on your breath, your body, and your senses. Notice how you feel in this moment, the surrounding sounds, and the colours and textures of the surrounding objects. Bring acceptance to all that is within and around you.

Everyday Mindfulness Exercises for Clients

There are many opportunities in everyday life to develop mindfulness. Here are few ways that you could suggest to your clients to practice mindfulness every day.

- Choose an everyday task, be it washing the dishes, having a shower, eating, driving to work, catching public transportation, brushing teeth, or cooking. Focus on the bodily senses as they go through this daily task.

- Walking to a meeting, focus on the feet, body, breathing, and emotions as they move toward the next meeting.

- Taking a mindful walk to the kitchen when feeling overwhelmed by work. Mindfully making a cup of tea and then drinking it mindfully before returning to their work desk.

- Mindful listening in meetings, focusing on being present, listening to the other person speak, and expressing themselves, noticing their feelings and senses as they listen.

- Setting up reminders, every hour or throughout the day to stop for one minute, focus on their breathing and body, closing their eyes and sensing how they are feeling.

- Use routine moments as reminders. For example, when you get into the car, go to bed, get up in the morning, have a cup of tea or coffee, use these everyday moments as reminders to spend a few moments practicing mindfulness.

- Setting an intention for the day: as they begin the day, they could set an intention to be mindful.

- Anchoring attention: focus on the breath, hands or feet as a way of focusing attention and practicing noticing when their attention wanders and bringing it back to the focus point.

- Taking a mindful walk outdoors when work and life gets overwhelming.

- Spending time with kids or pets – since they are effortlessly present most of the time, they provide an easy way to support adults to be mindful.

- Turn off distractions. Make sure email doesn't beep every time they receive an email. Turn off the phone for blocks of time.

- Schedule blocks of time to focus on one task at a time, being mindful as they complete the task, rather than getting distracted. Letting others know they can't be distracted and when they will be available.

- Pause before replying to emails or picking up the phone. Take a moment to be present so they can be fully present as they write the email or talk on the phone.

- Taking a break during the day to mindfully eat lunch. Stepping away from the office and focusing on being mindful as they eat.

- Pick a habit they want to change and for a period of time bring mindfulness to the habit without attempting to change it. Then bring mindfulness to what happens when they start to change the habit.

- Notice aversions and cravings during the day. For example, noticing an aversion every time the boss approaches their desk or every time they crave praise or attention from the boss.

- Start a mindfulness group at work. Support each other by setting times to meet and practice mindfulness for 10 minutes at a time, or agree to practice mindfulness for one minute at the beginning of each of the team meetings.

- Create time in the morning to mindfully arrive at work, rather than rushing into the office. Starting the day with mindfulness creates more likelihood that the day will be mindful.

- When giving feedback or experiencing conflict with someone else, bring mindfulness to what is happening for them internally before responding or reacting to what the other person is saying or doing.

- Bringing attention to the body, emotions, and inner dialogue when presenting to an audience. Notice what emotions arise, what happens in the body, like the heart beating fast, breathing shallow, and so on.

Every situation in the workplace can become a mindfulness practice. Whether it is conflict, managing time, giving feedback, communicating or meetings.

Creating a Mindfulness Group

One of the best ways clients can support themselves to practice mindfulness is to create a mindfulness group. Here is a process for setting up a mindfulness group at work:

1. **Information Session**

   - Invite others along to the 1-hour information session, giving a brief overview of the presentation.

   - Cover the following topics: what is mindfulness, the scientific benefits of mindfulness, how to practice mindfulness, and go through a mindfulness practice (e.g., body scan), ask others to share their experiences, cover both formal and informal practice, as well as the challenges of practicing mindfulness.

   - Share your own experience of practicing mindfulness (i.e., a practical application within the workplace).

   - Send out readings afterward, related to the benefits.

2. **Regular Group Mindfulness Practice**

- Set up a regular time each week - 30 minutes to an hour.

- Plan to meet the same time each week (e.g., lunchtime Friday).

- Find a meeting room that is quiet.

- Ask everyone to be on time.

- Set a structure, e.g. mindfulness practice, sharing experiences, and Q & A.

- Guide them through a mindfulness practice, e.g. use audio recording or guide participants through using your own words; leave some silence afterwards and then bring participants back from the practice with bells.

- Share a different mindfulness practice each week.

- Ask participants to share what they have learned about mindfulness after the practice and answer any questions.

- Ask participants to set an intention or action for the following week, for example, practicing daily, being mindful in team meetings or taking a moment to be mindful before answering the phone.

3. **Support Momentum**

- Send weekly reminders and articles to read about mindfulness.

- Choose a different theme for each week or month (e.g., mindfulness in the workplace, relationships, creativity, innovation, decision-making, leadership, etc.).

- Create an online forum to share experiences.

- Organise a questionnaire before and after eight weeks to measure the results of practicing mindfulness in the workplace (e.g., stress levels, pressure, and emotional reactions using, for example, a mindfulness questionnaire).

- Share information on apps (e.g., Insight Timer tells you when others are practicing mindfulness).

CHAPTER 9

MANAGING PROGRESS AND ACCOUNTABILITY

Mindfully Managing Progress

Coaches often set actions or homework for clients based on what they think the client should do to move forward, toward his or her desired outcomes. This approach can be useful at times, especially if the client is learning a new skill or being mentored by you in some way. However, it means the client is following the coach's agenda or what the coach thinks works best based on their experience, rather than trusting and following the client's energy. What has worked for us as coaches, won't necessarily work for the client.

For example, I remember years ago coaching a client who wanted to get fit and healthy. Based on my experience, I could have suggested going to a group training session, which I enjoy and have had great success with. However, what was going to work for this client was to have dancing lessons. She ended up competing in ballroom dancing competitions, was able to easily lose weight, get fit, strong, and happy, and meet a lot of new people. As a bonus, she also ended up satisfying another goal when she started a relationship with one of her dance partners.

This approach is about trusting the client to connect with their experience and then creating actions that will inspire and move them easily into action. It is about holding space for that connection and trusting that the relationship will bring forth the client's ability to find the best approach to move forward.

It is also about focusing more on creating a new awareness, rather than the 'how' or 'what' the client needs to do to take action. Coaches can often be so focused on getting their clients into action that they miss the insights or new awareness, and thus the actions become less effective, or the client has to work harder to implement the actions, rather than being led through inspiration.

For example, I recently had a client who was avoiding taking action on a creative project. She was able to think of actions to move forward however she felt like she 'should' take these actions rather than feeling inspired to action. Instead, I supported her to connect with herself in the present moment - particularly with her felt sense - and the creative impulse she felt at times. By focusing on this aspect, she had an insight that she was focusing on the result of the creative project and whether it would be meaningful to others, rather than the joy of creating.

She acknowledged the filter that had dampened down this creative energy, gave it space, and allowed it to be there with acceptance. In doing this, she was able to feel excited about creating again.

We let go of having to get into action and allowed it to come naturally from the unfolding of the present moment awareness. Inspired action is likely to arise naturally from the insights in the session, rather than client needing to think too hard about finding a solution. The actions come from an internal space rather than an external thinking about what the client should be doing.

Designing Mindful 'Who' Actions

Coaches often support clients to set actions based on the 'what'. What does the client need to do to affect the situation? For example: Talk to my boss about the project, create a vision board, look up websites for a leadership course, attend a course on how to engage my team, have a conversation with my husband, etc. It is also useful to support the client to set actions around the 'who'. What will support the client to shift 'who' they are being in the situation? What are they learning about themselves from this conversation? Based on this new awareness what action would they like to take? The action is more internally rather than externally focused.

For example, a client who wants to shift from being overly critical and negatively focused with her direct reports to being encouraging, engaging and allowing them to make mistakes. The 'what' actions could be to give each person on the team positive feedback at least once a week, to send positive client feedback to the wider group, so the team gets publicly acknowledged and to only check in with the team once a week instead of daily micromanaging them. These are useful actions and will likely move the client forward.

What would also be useful are some more internally focused actions about who she is being and who she wants to be with her team. She becomes aware during the session that she needs to shift her internal focus when talking to each of direct reports from being focused on the negative to the positive. So she also designs an action about being mindful (of her feelings, thoughts, body sensations) next time she has a meeting with her direct reports and then writing about it afterwards.

At the next meeting with the team, she becomes aware of a high level of tension in her body, and her heart is contracted. She notices her thoughts focus in on looking for what is wrong in what each person is saying. Then she goes into thinking about how she can fix it and has stopped listening fully. She makes assumptions and doesn't give her team space to explore new ideas. Instead, she jumps in with criticism and what she sees as a better way to approach the situation.

With this new awareness, she can then start to create an internal shift. For example, when she is in a meeting with the team and notices the tension in her body, instead of acting on it and pointing out what is wrong, she can focus on using mindfulness to relax, listening fully and then responding from this relaxed space.

It is useful to focus on setting actions based on the 'what' and 'who', as well as using mindfulness to shift their internal space. This internal shift is what creates the long-term sustainable results for the client.

Challenging Clients to Make Progress

Your work is not to drag the world kicking and screaming into a new awareness. Your job is to simply do your work...Sacredly, Secretly, and Silently... and those with 'eyes to see and ears to hear', will respond.

– The Arcturians

Coaches often challenge their clients to make progress. I see coaches trying to do this, feeling as if they have to, but noticing how the client seems to move into a contracted space instead of remaining open to learning. Sometimes, the client isn't even aware of this change. The client might even start referring to the coach as the expert, rather than trusting themselves.

Even the word 'challenge' can imply resistance to something, a pushing, rather than an allowing. Mindfulness is about openness, acceptance, and non-judgment. It is an allowing space, rather than a resistant space. Creating resistance gives the client something to push back against, which means that, as coaches, we have created barriers to new awareness.

I had an experience in the first few years of being coached by a very experienced coach. At one point in the conversation, she interrupted and said, 'You're not willing to own your strength.' Now, this admittedly sent me into a limbic response. I was stuck for words at the time, went into shock, and instead of being able to let in what the coach had said, I found excuses and withdrew my energy. Although there was truth in this statement, I wasn't able to let it in because of the way it had been delivered.

The reason that clients might go into a subtle form of limbic arousal is that when the coach challenges the client, she plugs into the client's already active inner judge dialogue. The coach is often unconsciously articulating what the client's inner judge probably says about her every day. In the above example, I discovered that my inner judge is often critical of me for being weak and not being strong enough. When I heard this comment from the coach, I went straight into an unconscious dialogue of 'See, you're not strong, you're weak'. I felt weak, powerlessness, and disempowered in that moment. I rejected how I felt and also rejected the comment from the coach.

It is possible to challenge a client without sending them into this limbic response. We need to look at our underlying intentions when challenging the client. To be aware of our intentions we need to bring mindfulness to our current moment experience when we feel the inclination to challenge the client. We need to be honest with ourselves about our intentions - if the intention is to prove your value or that you are the expert, then you are acting to satisfy your agenda, rather than the clients.

Through awareness, we can drop the identification our agenda and be present with the client instead. By listening deeply, we can share in the moment from a space of empowering the client. This way, the challenge becomes more like a stretch. The holding space of the session allows the client to stretch out of their comfort zone. However, it feels like they are doing it safely, within the session.

Inner Judge Attack

After clients have challenged themselves to go outside their comfort zones, there is often an 'inner judge backlash'. The inner judge berates them, either consciously or unconsciously, so they naturally feel the need to retreat into their comfort zones. This backlash is the main reason clients often have great success, but then suddenly, for no apparent reason, they retreat into old habits or sabotage themselves.

I had a client who worked for many years as a small business entrepreneur. She had moderate success and was ready to take it to a new level. She ran training programs for small businesses on branding. She had success working with clients one-on-one but didn't have as much success with participants enrolling in training programs. After working together for a while, she started to have more success and was almost selling out her programs. At first, she felt happy with her success. However, she also noticed she was becoming more and more anxious. She noticed that there would be problems with participants after she would start a program, and she would lose the energy to promote the next one.

She was sabotaging her success on an unconscious level. She became aware that holding the space for a larger group and the amount of financial gain she received was too much for her. It wasn't comfortable, so she would do subtle things that would make sure she wasn't as successful in the future. She noticed her cash flow would go up one month in a record month and the next few months would be well below the average she had established over the years. She felt as if she was going back to that average because it was safe. She started to feel tired of challenging herself to achieve new levels, and her inner judge attacked her in a way that would ensure she went back to the safety of the old ways of being.

Without the awareness of the underlying the situation, she likely would have continued pushing and trying to take action without success. However, by developing awareness of the 'inner judge backlash', she was able to take steps to gradually get used to holding the space for a larger group and financial abundance. It took time. However, she slowing increased her average income until she had tripled her income, which became the norm.

Bringing Mindfulness to Accountability

Often coaches take on the responsibility for keeping clients accountable. However, it is more effective when clients are ultimately responsible for keeping themselves accountable. When we become more aware and connected with ourselves internally, we become more responsible and are thus accountable to ourselves; we no longer need external accountability. Instead, what is needed is someone to support us, to check in with what is happening, and help us to create new insights about where we disconnect or sabotage ourselves.

The best question in this area you can ask a client is 'How can you keep yourself accountable?' The client can then create methods for keeping themselves accountable that aren't reliant on you having to be there - perhaps with friends and colleagues, but also with themselves, such as checking off a list, reminders in their schedule, keeping a journal, and so on.

How they keep themselves accountable will depend on the action they have set for themselves. If there is enough new awareness created in a conversation, then this will often propel the client to take action without the need for someone else to keep them accountable. The client will feel more empowered when they discover they can keep themselves accountable, and that they're responsible for taking action.

MINDFULNESS PRACTICE TRANSCRIPTS

The following transcripts can be used to guide clients through a mindfulness practice. I would suggest reading through the script a few times before using it with a client. You could even record yourself going through the script, so you can hear what works and doesn't work.

Make sure you pace yourself as you go through the practice. Allowing space and silence, so the client can feel and sense themselves. Stay present as you read and sense intuitively when you feel to add or take something out. Eventually, you will be able to let go of the script and create your own mindfulness practice to guide the client.

Focus on the Breath

Begin by finding a comfortable position for your body. Close your eyes and take a deep breath, inhaling deeply and exhaling. Begin to allow yourself to relax, going inside, beginning to slow down and relax. If sleepiness arises, give yourself a gentle message to stay alert and attentive, alert and aware as you relax and go inside.

Now, allow your attention to focus on your breath. Begin to watch your breathing. Notice how it enters and leaves the body, completely beyond your control, entering and leaving totally on its own. Watching the breath, feel yourself falling into its natural rhythm, coming in and going out on its own, each moment a new breath, coming in and going out, rising and falling.

The goal of this practice is to experience the breath without directing or changing it, to simply become aware of how the breath breathes itself, in its own rhythms.

You will start to notice that the mind wanders off easily. You may tell yourself to stay on the breath, however, the mind has a habit of wandering into thoughts about what you will do after the practice or other topics you feel you need to think about. Instead of giving the thoughts energy, gently bring yourself back to the breath, let go of the thoughts, and return to the breath. This is how you train the mind to be in the moment.

Allow yourself to continue following the natural breath. Notice if it feels light, heavy, full, cool, or warm. Bring a sense of curiosity to your natural breath. Notice how the chest rises, how the belly fills up and deflates, the coolness or warmth as the breath enters and leaves through the nostrils.

If the mind distracts you, gently bring your attention back to the breath.

Continue following the natural breath for a few minutes, noticing when the mind wanders and gently bringing your attention back to the breath.

After a few minutes, slowly bring your attention back to the room you're in and the chair you're sitting on and gently open your eyes when you're ready. There is no rush - just allow yourself to come back when you feel ready.

Breathing to the Count of Four

Begin by finding a comfortable position for your body. Close your eyes and take a deep breath, inhaling deeply and exhaling. Begin to allow yourself to relax, going inside, beginning to slow down and relax. If sleepiness arises, give yourself a gentle message to stay alert and attentive, alert and aware as you relax and go inside.

Now, allow your attention to focus on your breath and begin to watch the breathing, noticing how it enters and leaves the body, completely beyond your control, entering and leaving, totally on its own. Watching the breath, feel yourself falling into its natural rhythm, coming in and going out on its own, each moment a new breath, coming in and going out, rising and falling.

Begin to expand the breath by counting in and out for 4 counts. So, breathing in: 1...2...3...4...until you can't take in another sip of air, and then breathing out: 1...2...3...and 4... and then letting go of every ounce of breath.

Repeat counting to 4, in and out, for a least a couple of minutes, or for as long as you feel necessary. As you progress, you might notice your body and nervous system slowing relaxing with each breath.

Notice if your mind wanders from counting and gets distracted and gently bringing the mind back to the breath and counting again.

When you're ready, slowly bring your attention back to the room you're in and the chair you're sitting on and gently open your eyes. There is no rush, just allow yourself to come back when you feel ready.

Body Scan

Begin by finding a comfortable position for your body. Close your eyes and take a deep breath, inhaling deeply and exhaling. Begin to allow yourself to relax, going inside, beginning to slow down and relax. If sleepiness arises, give yourself a gentle message to stay alert and attentive, alert and aware as you relax and go inside.

Allow your attention to focus on your breath and begin to watch the breathing. Noticing how it enters and leaves the body completely beyond your control. Entering and leaving totally on its own. And watching the breath, begin to feel yourself falling into its natural rhythm, coming in and going out on its own. Each moment a new breath, coming in and going out, rising and falling.

Now, allow your attention to focus on your breath and begin to watch the breathing, noticing how it enters and leaves the body, completely beyond your control, entering and leaving, totally on its own. Watching the breath, feel yourself falling into its natural rhythm, coming in and going out on its own, each moment a new breath, coming in and going out, rising and falling.

We are now going to focus on different parts of the body. As we go through each part, notice the different sensations in this part of the body, whether it is heaviness, pain, lightness, itchiness, contraction, warmth, coolness and so on.

Start by focusing on the toes on your right foot, feeling into each of your toes and noticing any sensations. Then bring your attention to the front of the right foot, the back of the right foot, the right ankle, the right shin, the right calf muscle, the right knee, and the right thigh.

If you notice your mind moving away and getting distracted, gently bring your attention back to the body.

Then turn your attention to the left toes, the back of the left foot, the front of the left foot, the left ankle, the left shin, the left calf muscle, the left knee, and the left thigh.

If you notice your mind moving away and getting distracted, gently bring your attention back to the body.

Slowly bring your attention to the buttocks, the pelvis, the stomach, the lower chest, the upper chest, the lower back, the middle back, the upper back, and then the shoulders.

If you notice your mind moving away and getting distracted, gently bring your attention back to the body.

Turn your attention to the right arm, relaxing each of the fingers, then the back of the hand, the front of the hand, the wrist, the lower arm, the elbow, and the upper right arm.

If you notice your mind moving away and getting distracted, gently bring your attention back to the body.

Then the left hand, all the left fingers, and the thumb, the back of the hand, the front of the hand, the wrist, the lower arm, the elbow, and the left upper arm.

If you notice your mind moving away and getting distracted, gently bring your attention back to the body.

Then the shoulders and the neck, the chin, the cheeks, the nose, the eyes, the eyebrows, the forehead, the ears, the back of the head, and the crown of the head.

Then the whole body, from the crown of the head to the toes. Notice what others sensations capture your attention.

When you're ready, return your attention to the breath and bring your focus back into the room. Slowly open your eyes.

Exploring the Senses

Begin by finding a comfortable position for your body. Close your eyes and take a deep breath, inhaling deeply and exhaling. Begin to allow yourself to relax, going inside, beginning to slow down and relax. If sleepiness arises, give yourself a gentle message to stay alert and attentive, alert and aware as you relax and go inside.

Allow your attention to focus on your breath and begin to watch the breathing. Noticing how it enters and leaves the body completely beyond your control. Entering and leaving totally on its own. And watching the breath, begin to feel yourself falling into its natural rhythm, coming in and going out on its own. Each moment a new breath, coming in and going out, rising and falling.

Start by focusing on your sense of hearing. Open your ears and listen for any sounds that come into your awareness. For example, it might be somebody speaking, a bird singing, someone moving in your house, etc. The idea is to completely focus on this sense for a few minutes.

When you notice a sound, listen to it and then move onto another sound. There is no need to identify what the sound is. Instead, focus on the quality of the sound. Is it high-pitched or does it have a deeper sound? Really get curious about surrounding sounds.

See if you can listen for the faintest sound in your environment. Perhaps it is far away or nearby. There is no need to identify what the sound it is or where it comes from, simply notice it and then move on to see what else you can hear.

Notice when your mind wanders away and gently bring it back to the sounds in your environment. Continue focusing on listening to as many sounds as possible for a few minutes.

When you're ready, begin to focus on your sense of touch. Notice the feel of the fabric of your clothes, your shoes against your feet, the feel of the floor, and the feel of the air on your skin; is the air cool or warm? The idea is to get really curious about this sense and become aware of the sensation of anything touching your skin.

Notice if the mind wanders and gently bring your attention back to your sense of touch. Keep focusing on your sense of touch for a couple of minutes.

Next, bring your attention to your sense of taste. Notice how your mouth feels and what you can taste. Feel your tongue, the upper part of your mouth, the lower part of your mouth, and notice any taste sensations. You can even move your tongue around your mouth to feel what this is like.

Then bring your attention to your sense of smell. Notice what you can smell in your environment. You might not smell anything to start with, but keep focusing to see what might arise.

Notice if the mind wanders and gently bring your attention back to your sense of smell.

Start focusing on your body and your physical sensations. Notice wherever your attention takes you, but stay focused on the body. If you find your mind drifting away, then bring it back to the body. Be curious and open to different sensations in the body. It might be that you feel lightness, heaviness, pain, a tingling sensation, warmth, or coolness. Notice the sensations and move onto another part of the body. Notice if the mind attaches to the sensation. Gently bring the mind back to the body and then move to a different part of the body.

Continue focusing on the body for a couple of minutes.

When you're ready, open your eyes and focus on your visual sense. Start looking around the room, noticing the different objects, colours, textures, materials, light, shadows, and whatever else you can sense with your sight. Simply notice it and then move on, looking at different aspects of the room. The idea is to get really curious about this sense and be aware of what you're really looking at.

Explore for a few minutes. When you're ready to complete the mindfulness practice, remember to bring this awareness of your senses into your everyday life.

Focusing on an Object

Begin by finding a comfortable position for your body. Close your eyes and take a deep breath, inhaling deeply and exhaling. Begin to allow yourself to relax, going inside, beginning to slow down and relax. If sleepiness arises, give yourself a gentle message to stay alert and attentive, alert and aware as you relax and go inside.

Allow your attention to focus on your breath and begin to watch the breathing. Noticing how it enters and leaves the body completely beyond your control. Entering and leaving totally on its own. And watching the breath, begin to feel yourself falling into its natural rhythm, coming in and going out on its own. Each moment a new breath, coming in and going out, rising and falling.

When you're ready, open your eyes and focus on an object that is directly in front of you - it might be a pen, glass, cup, candle, or something else. Choose something that is simple and won't trigger the mind to go into a story about it, preferably not a computer screen, phone, photo, or book; choose something simple.

Really look at the object as if it were the first time you've seen this object. What colour is it? Notice the light and dark shades of the object, the texture and the material of the object, and anything else that is particular about this object. The idea is to get really curious about what you see. Notice any shadows or light reflecting off the object.

Notice if the mind wanders or goes into a story about the object and gently bring your attention back to simply observing the object.

Also, be aware of body sensations, emotions, thoughts that arise as you observe the object.

Spend a few minutes really looking at the object. When you're ready to complete the mindfulness exercise, notice how you feel or any other sensations that arise simply from being totally present to this object.

Expanded Awareness

Begin by finding a comfortable position for your body. Close your eyes and take a deep breath, inhaling deeply and exhaling. Begin to allow yourself to relax, going inside, beginning to slow down and relax. If sleepiness arises, give yourself a gentle message to stay alert and attentive, alert and aware as you relax and go inside.

Start by noticing the space to the right side of you. Notice how it feels, notice its depth, its temperature, its width, and its height. Notice anything else you observe about the space on your right side.

If you notice your mind moving away and getting distracted, gently bring your attention back to the right side.

Next, bring your attention to the space on the left side of your body. Notice how it feels: notice its depth, its temperature, its width, and its height. Notice anything else you observe about the space on your left side.

If you notice your mind moving away and getting distracted, gently bring your attention back to the left side.

Then bring your attention to the space behind your body. Notice how it feels: notice its depth, its temperature, its width, and its height. Notice anything else you observe about the space behind you.

If you notice your mind moving away and getting distracted, gently bring your attention back to the space behind you.

Bring your attention to the space in front of your body. Notice how it feels: notice its depth, the temperature, the width, and height of the space in front of you. Notice anything you observe about the space in front of your body.

If you notice your mind moving away and getting distracted, gently bring your attention back to the space in front of your body.

Next, bring your attention to the space above your body. Notice how it feels: notice its depth, its temperature, its width, and its height. Notice anything else you observe about the space above you.

If you notice your mind moving away and getting distracted, gently bring your attention back to the space above your body.

Then bring your attention to the space below your body. Notice how it feels: notice its depth, its temperature, its width, and its height. Notice anything else you observe about the space below your body.

If you notice your mind moving away and getting distracted, gently bring your attention back to the space below your body.

Bring your attention to the space all around your body and notice how this feels. When you're ready to bring yourself back, slowly open your eyes.

Mindful Eating

This exercise can be done anytime you eat something. The purpose is to bring mindful awareness to everything you eat and use all of your senses. It is best done without any distractions like TV, reading, or talking. Instead, focus on eating quietly and mindfully without interruption.

Before starting to eat, close your eyes for a few moments to feel your breath, your body, and how you feel in this moment. Bring your attention to your breath and take in a few deep breaths if needed, so you can start to relax your nervous system.

When you feel relaxed and mindful, open your eyes and start to open up all of your senses. Notice, in particular, how the food smells and what it looks like. Notice the different colours, textures, lights and shadows of the food. Spend a couple of minutes smelling and observing the food before eating.

When you're ready, slowly, mindfully start to eat. Notice how the food tastes and chew slowly so you can fully taste the food.

Notice if the mind wanders or wants to hurry the process of eating. Instead, focus on chewing slowly, noticing the taste and sensation of the food. Try to eat even more slowly than you feel is possible.

Take your time eating the food, then notice how you feel after eating. You will likely notice that it was a much more enjoyable experience, especially if it was something yummy, like a mango or piece of chocolate! Or you might notice that sensation of eating was unpleasant. Remember to bring mindful acceptance to whatever arises.

Noticing the World Around You

This practice can be done whenever you walk down a street, in nature, standing in a queue somewhere, sitting on a bus, or even at your desk or walking around the office. The purpose is to bring awareness to everything surrounding you, using all your senses.

As you walk, start by bringing your attention to your thoughts. Notice if the mind wanders and ruminates about the past or future and gently bring your attention back to the surrounding environment.

Start by noticing the footpath or road you're walking on. Notice the dirt, the concrete, and cracks in the path; notice the light and shadows, the gutters, the colours, and anything else you observe about the footpath or road.

Next, bring your attention to the surrounding buildings. Notice the colours, shadows, light, textures, shapes, materials, and anything else you observe about the buildings.

Notice if your mind wanders to thoughts about the past or future and bring your attention gently back to the world around you.

Bring your attention to nature, the trees, plants, grass, and/or flowers around you. Notice the colours, the textures, the movement of the plants and/or trees, the wind as it moves the plants and/or trees, the shadows, the light reflecting off the plants and/or trees, and anything else you notice about the scenery around you.

Then bring your attention to the sky. Notice the clouds, the light, the dark, the colour of the sky, and anything else you observe.

Also notice the surrounding sounds: people talking, trees rustling, traffic, birds, and any other sounds you notice.

Notice, also, how the people around you look, what are they wearing, their facial expressions, body language, and anything else you observe about the people around you. Continue focusing in this way as you go about your day instead of getting lost in your thoughts. Notice the difference you feel.

Repetitive Tasks (Washing the Dishes)

This mindfulness practice can be done with any everyday repetitive task like washing the dishes, brushing your teeth, cleaning the house, having a shower, or whatever daily task you choose. It is sometimes useful to choose a task with which you know you tend to be less mindful and perhaps resent having to do.

For this exercise, we will choose washing the dishes. Start by taking a moment to close your eyes and feel your body, noticing particular sensations in the body. Notice how you feel and label some of your emotions (e.g., resentment, joy, happiness, anger, etc.). Allow yourself to fully feel your emotions without going into a story about what happened; simply feel.

When you're ready to start washing dishes, open up your senses. Notice the smells of the washing liquid or leftover food. Notice the colour of the dishes and how the dishes feel as you wash them, the feel of the water against your skin, the way the water falls off the dishes, or the suds that stick to them.

Notice the temperature of the water: is it really hot, warm, or cold. Also, notice how your body feels and the different emotions that arise. Feel your feet on the ground. Notice the texture and feel of the clothes you're wearing.

You might also notice the sounds of the dishes as they are washed, the sound of the water running, or any other sounds in your environment.

Notice if your mind starts to wander into thoughts about the future or past and bring your attention gently back to the washing of the dishes and your senses.

Keep being mindfully aware of all your senses as you wash the dishes. Develop the mind of the observer, watching everything including your thoughts as they come in to distract you from being completely in the moment as you wash the dishes. Notice how you feel afterward.

Open Presence with Bells

For this practice you will need to record some bells at 1-2 minute intervals or use an App like Insight Timer[21] - allows you to set bells to ring at whatever interval you choose.

In this practice, you will allow your attention to notice whatever captures your attention. The purpose is to bring an observer's mind to your surroundings and your body sensations, feelings, thoughts, and other senses. Allow your presence and awareness to open up to and observe everything. Then when you hear the bells, this will alert you to come back, to focus in the moment, if your mind has wondered.

Begin by finding a comfortable position for your body. Close your eyes and take a deep breath, inhaling deeply and exhaling. Begin to allow yourself to relax, going inside, beginning to slow down and relax. If sleepiness arises, give yourself a gentle message to stay alert and attentive, alert and aware as you relax and go inside.

Allow your attention to focus on your breath and begin to watch your breathing. Notice how it enters and leaves your body, completely beyond your control, entering and leaving, totally on its own. Watching the breath, feel yourself fall into its natural rhythm, coming in and going out on its own. Each moment a new breath, coming in and going out, rising and falling.

Allow your attention to notice whatever arises in your experience. You might notice how your body feels, particular bodily sensations, emotions, sounds, thoughts, the feeling of your clothes on your skin, the temperature of surrounding air, smells, or anything else that captures your attention.

21 https://insighttimer.com/

The idea is to simply notice each sensation, emotion or thought without analysing. If you find yourself starting to think and analyse, then bring your awareness to this tendency. Don't make yourself feel wrong for going into these thoughts. Instead, bring your attention gently back to awareness in the moment.

Keep allowing your presence to open and observe everything. When you hear the bells, notice if you're lost in a thought and bring your attention to the thought and the present moment.

When you're ready to begin preparing yourself to come back, slowly open your eyes.
